DAY TRIPS
FROM EDMONTON

BEST OF ALBERTA
DAY TRIPS
FROM EDMONTON

Joan Marie Galat

whitecap

Cover design: Mauve Pagé and
Marjolein Visser
Cover photos: © iStockphoto.com/Northern
Photo (bison and Elk Island); © iStockphoto
.com/Imagine Golf (grain elevator);
© iStockphoto.com/Weygan Randy Mayes
(Edmonton skyline); Town of Stony Plain
(mural entitled *Making a Friend*)
Editing: Brendan Wild
Interior design: Mauve Pagé and Warren Clark
Maps: Leslie Bell | www.lesliebell.com
Proofreading: Lesley Cameron
Uncredited photos are courtesy of the author.

Printed in Canada by Webcom.

**Library and Archives Canada
Cataloguing in Publication**

Galat, Joan Marie, 1963–
        Day trips from Edmonton / Joan Marie
Galat.

Includes index.
ISBN 978-1-55285-985-8

        1. Edmonton Region
(Alta.)—Guidebooks.
2. Alberta—Guidebooks. I. Title.

FC3657.G35 2009   917.123'34044
C2008-905581-0

The publisher acknowledges the financial
support of the Government of Canada
through the Book Publishing Industry
Development Program (BPIDP) and the
Province of British Columbia through the
Book Publishing Tax Credit.

09 10 11 12 13   5 4 3 2 1

For Grant, who packs the best picnics
and makes every trip an adventure

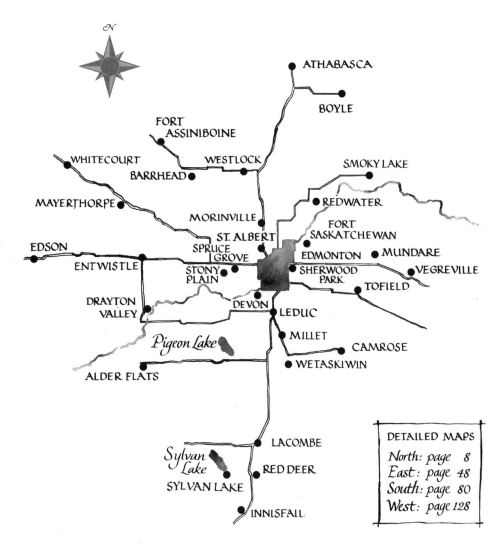

ATHABASCA

BOYLE

FORT
ASSINIBOINE

WESTLOCK

WHITECOURT

BARRHEAD

SMOKY LAKE

MAYERTHORPE

MORINVILLE

REDWATER

EDSON

ST. ALBERT

SPRUCE
GROVE

FORT
SASKATCHEWAN

ENTWISTLE

EDMONTON

MUNDARE

STONY
PLAIN

SHERWOOD
PARK

VEGREVILLE

DRAYTON
VALLEY

DEVON

LEDUC

TOFIELD

Pigeon Lake

MILLET

CAMROSE

ALDER FLATS

WETASKIWIN

LACOMBE

*Sylvan
Lake*

RED DEER

SYLVAN LAKE

INNISFAIL

DETAILED MAPS

North: page   8
East: page 48
South: page 80
West: page 128

CONTENTS

EAST OF EDMONTON

SOUTH OF EDMONTON

INTRODUCTION

There are many perks to taking a day trip. You don't need to pack an overnight bag, find someone to water your plants, or arrange for someone to pick up your mail. It's not necessary to win the lottery, cash in frequent flyer points, or start searching for lost savings accounts to finance a trip. You won't have to work overtime to bank weeks of extra days off, and you won't be gone long enough to miss your loved ones or any pets who can't come along for the ride. All you need is a reliable form of transportation, a full tank of gas, this guide, and perhaps a picnic. Day trips have always appealed to me for all these reasons.

An Alberta resident for many years, I have lived in various areas but always within a few hours of Edmonton. In that time I have spent many hours on the road and frequently found occasions to seek out the pleasure of fresh wonders along the way—all while indulging a rather persistent passion for picnicking. Writing this book has given me the opportunity to share these discoveries.

During my travels I have contemplated the general tendency many of us have: we take long trips in search of the unusual and interesting while disregarding many fascinating points of interest close to home. Perhaps it's a habit to assume anything worth seeing is far, far away. For those living in the Edmonton area, what a happy surprise to discover a multitude of treasures close to home. Use this guide the next time you want to treat yourself to a day off, entertain out-of-town guests, or go on a date that offers something more original than supper and a movie. Take a day trip to teach your children Alberta history, and show them why they should feel pride in Alberta's wonders. For those visiting from more distant locales, *Day Trips from Edmonton* will reveal parts of the province where early pioneers thrived as they made their mark in Canada. These intriguing sites in Alberta towns, cities, and country spaces are all just a road trip and picnic away.

All the sites described in *Day Trips from Edmonton* lie within a two-hour drive from Edmonton's downtown. I have included natural wonders, human-engineered points of interest, historic sites, cultural features, museums, picnic spots, and recreational opportunities. In addition, I have described seasonal opportunities to highlight the appeal of sites throughout the year, so do not limit yourself to thinking day trips are only a summertime activity. The sites within Edmonton's day-trip range can be enjoyed any time of year. They bring surprising new delights when experienced in different seasons and provide distinct opportunities to truly appreciate this area's multitude of features. There are many reasonably untouched places to explore and enjoy in solitude; there are also locations bustling with activities and events, including farmers' markets, rodeos, fairs, and parades, as well as festivals, outdoor concerts, and community-wide garage sales.

The two-hour circle around Edmonton encompasses a variety of habitats and spectacular multi-hued natural landscapes. You will see parkland where trembling aspen woods alternate with farmland, defining the transition zone between southern prairie and northern boreal forest. Fields may be golden yellow with canola, tan with barley or wheat, or green with one of the many garden crops grown in this region. You will pass pastures that are, respectively, grazed by a wide assortment of cattle, including the black and white Holstein and the red and white Hereford; there are also black Angus and red Angus, Black Baldies (which are usually a Hereford-Black Angus cross and are black with white faces), the usually sparkling white Charolais, the Simmental (with red and white patchy markings), and even some Belted Galloways (with a black-white-black pattern like an Oreo cookie on legs); and don't forget the horses, donkeys, bison, sheep, pigs, turkeys, and goats. Watch the farms for more exotic livestock such as elk, wild boar, game birds, alpacas, llamas, emus, and ostriches.

As you drive through rural Alberta, look for the grey and sagging pioneer homes and barns that still stand, sometimes surrounded by windbreaks of spruce or poplar. Imagine the first settlers arriving by cart and wagon, searching for land—generally seeking flat ground with some trees for lumber, as well as a grassy area and water source. Settlers chose their homesteads when much more of this area was forested, and judged the soil according to the trees they observed growing. Your travels will lead you through a mixture of parkland, rolling moraine, mixed-wood forest, muskeg, sandy pinewoods, and land gently rising toward the foothills. Much of this will be punctuated with wetlands and often preserved in parks and designated natural areas. It is interesting to learn that every Alberta provincial park and protected area has been designated for a specific reason. Each one safeguards a section of Alberta's diverse flora, fauna, and land features, and provides opportunities to enjoy outdoor recreation or experience the area's cultural heritage.

A provincial park or protected area can be found within about 100 kilometres, or just over an hour's drive, of every home in Alberta, and there are many within two hours of Edmonton. Mysteries of the boreal forest, as well as sand dunes, secluded lakes, and Klondike history, lie to the north, while the south offers numerous surprises nestled among the farmlands, including police dog training demonstrations, the home of an Icelandic poet, and lake resorts.

Just east of Edmonton, Elk Island National Park is a jewel of habitats, wildlife, and bison herds; unencumbered by light pollution, this is also Alberta's designated dark sky area for viewing celestial sites. Also east is Beaverhill Lake, one of only a few federally recognized Canadian bird sanctuaries.

To the city's immediate west lies the Wagner Natural Area—162 hectares (400 acres) of wilderness formed by a 5,000-year-old peatland

and rich spring fen. Famous for its plants, this area is home to a diverse range of orchids not found in the neighbouring parkland terrain. Farther west, the elevation gradually rises toward the Rocky Mountains, offering increasingly varied landscape and features to investigate.

Small towns, lakes, rivers, white sand beaches, fossil beds, and historic sites are scattered among the trembling aspen forests and farmland that make up the parkland ecosystem. There are opportunities to enjoy walks, hikes, or bike rides, as well as to go boating, tubing, swimming, wading, fishing, and birding. Your prospects for viewing wildlife are exceedingly high, especially if you develop the habit of scanning fields, forest edges, and highway ditches, particularly during twilight hours.

Winter provides the chance to spot waterfowl and birds of prey west of Edmonton, where the operation of power plants keeps parts of Wabamun Lake ice-free year-round. The snowy season also offers fine cross-country ski trails, toboggan runs, snowshoeing, and outdoor skating—and even polar dips for the very hardy.

The area covered in *Day Trips from Edmonton* contains ecological reserves that protect specific habitats and their associated biodiversity, including rare and fragile landscapes, plants, animals, and geological features. Areas defined as ecological reserves are set aside for strict preservation, with access typically allowed only on foot, and with activities limited to harmless and unobtrusive pastimes such as photography, astronomy, and wildlife viewing.

Provincial parks offer a great range of outdoor recreational opportunities combined with good road access. They often host interpretive programs that highlight an area's natural heritage and aim to serve visitors of diverse interests, ages, physical abilities, and skill.

Provincial recreation areas offer outdoor pursuits in natural and engineered settings in landscapes that may or may not be developed. You can expect to find picnic tables, firepits, drinking water, toilet facilities, and garbage containers in provincial parks and recreation areas. Many also have picnic or cooking shelters.

Natural areas include natural and near-natural landscapes that have local significance for use in nature-based recreation and heritage appreciation. Typically small, they usually do not provide any facilities beyond parking areas and trails.

The zone around Edmonton also offers much in the way of pioneer, early settler, and Aboriginal history. You will find historic sites, restored homesteads, renovated schoolhouses, grain elevators, pioneer museums, and interpretive centres. These explain local history and, in some locations, are populated with costumed interpreters.

You can see where oil was first discovered, what tools Alberta's first farmers used, early weaponry, fur-trading posts, and missionary centres. The Ukrainian Cultural Heritage Village portrays Ukrainian pioneers' everyday experiences in a community of historic buildings surrounded by wheat and canola fields that shimmer beneath the blazing prairie sun.

The history of transportation comes alive at the Reynolds-Alberta Museum in Wetaskiwin, where an extensive collection of vehicles, aircraft, tractors, and heavy equipment will astound anyone who appreciates the modern conveniences available to today's day tripper.

No matter what roads you choose to travel—whether close to Edmonton's city limits or farther afield—you will find the trips within a two-hour radius of Edmonton's city centre offer exciting opportunities for holidays close to your home base. The directions that follow provide you with places to begin your adventures and all the information you need to veer off at any point in pursuit of your favourite activities.

ONE-OF-A-KIND ATTRACTIONS

Seek out the unique! The Edmonton area's most singular
and memorable attractions and landmarks define Alberta communities,
while offering special appeal to the day tripper.

BEST PLACES FOR BIRDERS

Stalk a flock at these rich bird havens. Whether you see an avian assembly
with familiar feathers or spot one of those much sought-after species,
you are likely to find a habitat you want to explore more than once.

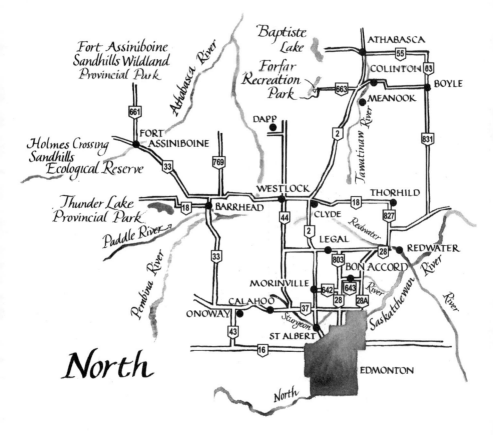

Fort Assiniboine
Sandhills Wildland
Provincial Park

Athabasca River

Baptiste Lake

Forfar Recreation Park

ATHABASCA

55

COLINTON

83

BOYLE

661

663

MEANOOK

DAPP

FORT ASSINIBOINE

2

831

Holmes Crossing Sandhills Ecological Reserve

33

769

WESTLOCK

THORHILD

Tawatinaw River

Thunder Lake Provincial Park

18

BARRHEAD

44

CLYDE

18

827

Paddle River

2

Redwater

Pembina River

33

LEGAL

28

REDWATER

803

BON ACCORD

River

Saskatchewan River

MORINVILLE

642

643

River

CALAHOO

37

28

28A

ONOWAY

43

Sturgeon

ST ALBERT

North

16

EDMONTON

North

NORTH OF EDMONTON

There are so many interesting things to see north of Edmonton, you may choose to make a loop of your journey or to take several trips to various point destinations. The northern routes include St. Albert, Morinville, and Legal, with their strong Roman Catholic missionary history, and encompass sites such as Mission Hill, Father Lacombe Chapel, and St. Jean-Baptiste Church. The north is also home to Lois Hole Centennial Provincial Park, which is Alberta's 69th provincial park and an officially designated Important Bird Area.

The Westlock, Barrhead, Fort Assiniboine, and Athabasca areas are rich in recreational opportunities, as well as pioneer and Klondike history. The Athabasca Landing Trail, walking history jaunts, and Alberta Pacific Forestry Industries tours rival the sorts of attractions you might be willing to drive much farther to see!

ST. ALBERT

Directions: Travel north on St. Albert Trail, which becomes Hwy 2. Watch for the Welcome to St. Albert sign—Edmonton and St. Albert are connected.
Distance: About 24 km, or 16 minutes, from downtown Edmonton.
Info: 780-459-1500; www.stalbert.ca.

A growing city on Edmonton's northwestern outskirts, St. Albert is an attractive bedroom community for Edmonton employees, and its population continues to increase. The city provides services for the

SIMPLE SUMMER FAMILY DAY TRIP
Total driving time: about 3 hours

For a fun family getaway on a Saturday, enjoy this mix of history, water fun, and pic-nicking. Make your first stop at the massive outdoor farmers' market in **downtown St. Albert**, on St. Anne and St. Thomas Streets (it's open from 10:00 a.m.to 3:00 p.m. every Saturday from July to September). Pick up some fresh picnic treats, then drive to **Mission Hill** (page 13) in St. Albert, where you can meander along the self-guided walk and visit Father Lacombe Chapel, Vital Grandin Centre, Father Lacombe statue, the Mis-sion Bells, crypt, Stations of the Cross, and a replica of a Lourdes grotto.

Depending on the age of children travelling with you, plan to picnic at the splash park in **Red Willow Park** (page 19) or have a late picnic lunch near Westlock at the **Edmonton Skydive Centre** (page 28) where you can watch parachutists practise their sport. Hop back in the car and go to **Long Island Lake Municipal Park** (page 29) to enjoy a variety of outdoor pursuits or just relax over a picnic, before heading home.

extensive farming area north of Edmonton and also has much to offer the day tourist. The Sturgeon River flows eastward through the city of St. Albert, eventually draining into the North Saskatchewan River. The slow and shallow Sturgeon River created the area's placid, rolling hills. The Sturgeon River is marked on David Thompson's 1814 map, although the Cree had another name for the river—*mi-koo-oo-pow,* meaning "red willow." Many sturgeon were once caught here.

More than 145 years ago, St. Albert became a settlement through the efforts of one of the first missionaries to come west. Father Albert Lacombe was an energetic member of the Missionary Oblates of Mary Immaculate. He wanted to minister to the Métis community formerly known as Big Lake and help them establish a farming lifestyle. He felt having a trace of Aboriginal blood helped endear him to Métis and Aboriginal peoples.

Before St. Albert became a Roman Catholic mission, many Métis tried to settle around Lac Ste. Anne, but the heavy soil, cool weather, and short growing season left them frustrated. In the early 1860s, Father Lacombe chose the area for a new missionary settlement, which Bishop A. Taché named St. Albert, after Father Lacombe's patron saint. The spot was chosen for its proximity to Fort Edmonton—only 14 kilometres away. The district's grassy hills, wooded areas, river, valley, and distant lake were also appreciated. The rich, black soil was easy to work with, and a forest fire had made the land easier to clear.

Spring of 1861 saw Father Lacombe, accompanied by a few Métis families, travel to the new site with four oxen, a few horses, a plow, and other tools. They brought a large bison skin tent to live in and use as a chapel until permanent buildings could be raised.

The new residents built houses, planted gardens, and constructed a bridge across the Sturgeon River. They built a horse-driven mill in 1863, but before long, replaced it with a water-powered mill. St. Albert grew quickly and became the largest community of farmers west of Winnipeg. The Grey Nuns moved from Lac Ste. Anne and set up a school in 1863, and settlers came from Quebec, creating one

RACHEL J. PHOTOGRAPHY

St. Albert grain elevators

of the largest French-language communities in Canada outside Quebec. The province's oldest non-fortified community, St. Albert was incorporated as a village in 1900, a town in 1904, and a city in 1977. Now almost 60,000 people live here. The city's rich Roman Catholic heritage is still apparent in its education system: Catholic schools are designated public schools, while separate schools are Protestant, offering non-denominational teaching.

The city's historic significance is enhanced with an artistic presence, as well as opportunities to enjoy the outdoors through 445 hectares (1,100 acres) of natural spaces and 34 kilometres of trails. Western Canada's largest outdoor farmers' market is held in downtown St. Albert every Saturday from July through September. Annual events include the International Children's Festival, Rock'n August Car Show and Music Festival, and Kinsmen Rainmaker Rodeo.

St. Albert Grain Elevator Park (SAGE Park), Train Station, and Visitor Centre

Location: At the corner of Mission Avenue and Meadowview Drive in St. Albert. While northbound on St. Albert Trail (Hwy 2), turn left at St. Anne Street, right at Perron Street, left at Mission Avenue, then left again at Meadowview Drive.
Info: Interpreters lead tours of the train station and historic grain elevators. Open from Victoria Day weekend until Labour Day, Wednesday to Sunday, 10 a.m. to 6 p.m. Admission by donation. 780-419-7354, or 780-459-1528 in the off-season.

Two wooden grain elevators reach for the sky in the St. Albert Grain Elevator Park—the place to learn about the area's agricultural history. Both the 1906 Alberta Grain Company Elevator and the 1929 Alberta Wheat Pool Elevator are recognized Provincial Historic Resources. The Rotary Train Station and Visitor Centre was built in 2005 as a replica of a 1920s station.

Mission Hill

Location: St. Vital Avenue, in St. Albert. If northbound on St. Albert Trail (Hwy 2), turn left on St. Vital Avenue.
Info: Always accessible. Pick up a guide at the Visitor Centre. 780-459-1724 (City of St. Albert).

Overlooking the scenic Sturgeon River valley and downtown St. Albert, the St. Albert Mission was founded on Mission Hill, where St. Albert Parish is now located. Take the self-guided walking tour and imagine how the landscape would have looked more than 100 years ago, covered with deciduous and evergreen forests and hunted for its numerous fur-bearing animals. You will see a number of historic sites, including Father Lacombe Chapel, Vital Grandin Centre, Father Lacombe statue, and the Mission Bells. The crypt that houses the remains of Bishop Grandin, Father Lacombe, and Father Leduc is located here, as are the Stations of the Cross and a replica of the grotto in Lourdes to honour the Blessed Virgin Mary.

Text on statue:

FATHER LACOMBE, O.M.I.

A MISSIONARY
& PIONEER
OF THE NORTHWEST.

UN MISSIONNAIRE
& PIONNIER
DU NORD-OUEST.

FOR 67 YEARS
HE LABORED
FOR GOD,
HIS FELLOWMEN
AND HIS COUNTRY.

PENDANT 67 ANS
IL SE DÉPENSA
POUR DIEU,
SON PROCHAIN
ET SON PAYS.

BORN IN QUEBEC
1827.

NÉ DANS QUÉBEC
1827.

RACHEL J. PHOTOGRAPHY

Father Lacombe statue on Mission Hill

Father Lacombe Chapel

Location: On Mission Hill, on St. Vital Avenue (see Mission Hill, page 13).
Info: Open May 15 to Labour Day daily from 10 a.m. to 6 p.m. Occasional special events include Sunday Fun Days on the first and third Sundays of the month, which portray the lifestyles of Alberta's early missionaries, settlers, and Métis. Admission charged. 780-459-7663; father.lacombe@gov.ab.ca.

Father Lacombe Chapel is the oldest building in Alberta and the heart of the original community. In 1861, the Métis built the unpretentious chapel on the high ground north of the Sturgeon River, using the post-on-sill style known in the west as Red River frame construction. In 1870, a terrible smallpox epidemic occurred, and the mission became a refuge for about 700 Métis and Aboriginal people. The same year, a larger church was built to serve as a cathedral. The chapel became a storage facility until 1929, when it was turned into the Father Lacombe Museum. An Alberta Provincial Historic Site, the Father Lacombe Chapel was restored to reflect its original appearance.

Interpreters who speak both English and French lead visitors on a fascinating tour of Father Lacombe Chapel, as well as the grotto, and the crypt holding Father Lacombe's and Bishop Grandin's tombs. You can see demonstrations of pioneer activities and walk through the cemetery where St. Albert's first families rest.

Locally known as the Bishop's Palace, Vital Grandin Centre is next to Father Lacombe Chapel. Built in 1887, this was the home of Vital Grandin, Alberta's first Catholic bishop. Born in northern France, Grandin spent most of his adult life in the northwestern areas that now define Saskatchewan and Alberta. Pope Pius IX installed him as head of the St. Albert Diocese in 1872. Although challenged with a speech impediment, Grandin still ministered to approximately 12,000 Aboriginal people, 5,000 Métis, and a few hundred whites in Alberta, Saskatchewan, and the Northwest Territories, assisted by only nine Oblate priests and a few brothers. He tackled many issues on behalf of his parishioners and was successful in many of his

RACHEL J. PHOTOGRAPHY

Father Lacombe Chapel

endeavours, including the building of schools, orphanages, and hospitals. In 1884 he acted as a mediator between the Métis and federal government in an unsuccessful attempt to prevent Louis Riel and other Métis leaders from participating in violent rebellion. Grandin died on June 3, 1902. In 1937, the Roman Catholic Church recognized his holy life and character with beatification. He was declared venerable in 1966.

Musée Héritage Museum

Location: St. Albert Place, 5 St. Anne Street, St. Albert. If northbound on St. Albert Trail (Hwy 2), turn left at St. Anne Street.
Info: Open 10 a.m. to 5 p.m. from Tuesday to Saturday, and 1 p.m. to 5 p.m. on Sunday. Closed statutory holidays. Admission is free; donations are welcome. 780-459-1528; museum@st-albert.net.

The Musée Héritage Museum tells St. Albert's natural and cultural history, with more than 6,500 artifacts that reveal how Aboriginals, Métis, and missionaries contributed to early settlement in the

St. Albert area. Housed in St. Albert Place, and designed by renowned Canadian architect Douglas Cardinal, the museum aims to appeal to visitors of all ages. A new exhibit is produced annually and hosts multiple travelling collections from around the world. Children will enjoy the interactive Discovery Room where themes change regularly. This museum is worthy of return visits.

Little White School

Location: 2 Madonna Drive, St. Albert. If northbound on St. Albert Trail (Hwy 2), turn left on St. Vital Avenue, and left again on Madonna Drive.
Info: Call ahead: 780-459-4404. Admission: donations are welcome.

The Little White School provides an engaging example of the early education experience. When the school first opened to students in 1948, the nearest water pump was a field away, and students used holes in the basement floor for toilets. The school was originally named the "Little" Father Jan School, after parish priest Father Alphonse Jan.

Lois Hole Centennial Provincial Park

Location: Travel north on St. Albert Trail (Hwy 2), turn left onto 137th Avenue (before entering the town of St. Albert), then right onto Sir Winston Churchill Avenue (184th Street), and left onto Levasseur Road, which becomes Riel Drive. Leave your vehicle at the St. Albert Rugby Football Club parking lot, or drive farther along Riel Drive and turn left on Rodeo Drive to reach the gravel parking lot by the gazebo.
Info: 780-960-8170.

Lois Hole Centennial Provincial Park contains the former Big Lake Natural Area—a shallow wetland surrounded by small deciduous and mixed coniferous woodlands. A centennial legacy, the park was established in 2005 to honour the late Lieutenant Governor's passion for Alberta youth, education, and the environment. Birdlife International, a worldwide partnership of non-government conservation organizations, recognizes Big Lake as an Important Bird Area. The lake provides essential bird habitat and is a major waterfowl moulting and staging area. You may find great numbers of tundra swans and Franklin's gulls here. Look for tundra swans during spring break-up in April and early May as they fly north to the still-frozen Arctic breeding grounds. Most fall migration occurs in October. One fall, the lake's bird population included 20,000 swans.

Big Lake is also designated a globally significant Important Bird Area because of the vast variety of species found here throughout the year. In the late 1990s, 10,000 northern pintails were recorded during spring migration. Osprey and bald eagle sightings are increasing, and Eurasian widgeons are spotted every year. Upon their return from southern Peru and northern Chile, Franklin's gulls settle in the western bay, where they attach floating nests to aquatic plants.

A threatened species, the peregrine falcon can be seen hunting in the park. Highly regarded for swift flight, grace, and splendour, these falcons were likely released as captive-bred young from the peregrine falcon reintroduction program in Edmonton. Watch for falcons along the shoreline at dawn and dusk as they hunt on the wing, capturing small perching birds, as well as larger species like ducks. Possibly the fastest of all birds, a peregrine falcon can dive at speeds near 320 kilometres per hour.

Big Lake is part of the 260-kilometre-long Sturgeon River system that flows east to the North Saskatchewan River. One of only three bird's-foot deltas in the province, its many distributaries extend outward to create the appearance of a bird claw.

Often mentioned in St. Albert history, Big Lake was important to settlers who hunted and fished, and also trapped beaver and muskrat. The community used the river and lake for drinking water well into the 1900s. Artifacts on the lake's eastern shore prove the presence of a primitive community 5,000 years ago, though archaeologists suspect nomadic people used Big Lake as early as 9,000 years ago. Archaeologists have found stone tools and weapons on the south and east sides of the lake.

CITY OF ST. ALBERT

Downtown St. Albert

Red Willow Park

Location: Access along Sturgeon Drive in St. Albert. Travel north on St. Albert Drive (Hwy 2). Turn right at Sturgeon Road, make a slight left to stay on Sturgeon Road, and turn left at Berrymore Drive.

Info: Trail maps are available at the tourist information centre. All dogs on trails must be leashed.

St. Albert Train Station Visitor Centre

Red Willow Park extends the full length of the Sturgeon River valley and contains 70 kilometres of walking trails. More than 34 kilometres are paved—perfect for inline skating, cycling, walking, or running. The trail system connects most of St. Albert's neighbourhood parks and includes five major parks—Lacombe Lake Park, Lions Park, St. Albert Place Promenade, Woodlands Park, and Kingswood Park.

If children are part of your day trip, Woodlands Water Spray Park on the banks of the Sturgeon River is one of the most fun places to visit. This is Canada's second interactive water area of this kind and was Western Canada's first spray park. In 2007, the splash zone was upgraded and reopened with a medieval theme. The spray zones are grouped roughly into three different age-appropriate sections, making it easier for toddlers and young children to play alongside older splashers. The park's new water treatment building maximizes the water's contact with chlorine and is used by Capital Health as a model for new spray parks. You will find picnic areas, sand volleyball, and a skate park.

Ted Hole Park, in the centre of St. Albert's Erin Ridge development, offers a natural environment for recreation and leisure activities. A paved walkway links the park with the Red Willow Park system. The late Lieutenant Governor Lois Hole and her late husband, Ted, owned and farmed the land where the park is located. It is a natural recreation spot with interpretive signs that identify local trees and animals; signs also explain the Hole family's contributions to St. Albert and Alberta.

St. Albert Botanic Park

Location: Access along Sturgeon Road in St. Albert. Travel north on St. Albert Drive (Hwy 2). Turn right onto Sturgeon Road and travel about 1 km to 265 Sturgeon Road. The park is 1 km east of Boudreau Road and is surrounded by Red Willow Park and the riverside trail system.
Info: Open year-round, with the best viewing from May through September. The John Beedle Centre is wheelchair accessible. Admission is free, with an honorarium suggested for group tours. 780-458-7163; www.stalbertbotanicpark.com; info@stalbertbotanicpark.com.

St. Albert Botanic Park encompasses 2 hectares (5 acres) along the scenic bank of the winding Sturgeon River—a brief walk east from St. Albert's city hall via Red Willow Trail. This is a beautiful place to inhale garden scents. If you can, return throughout the summer to repeat strolls through the gardens and see how the plants transform from blossom to seed through the growing season. The park specializes in garden flowers appropriate for St. Albert and Edmonton, and benches throughout the grounds provide lovely picnic spots and special places to share a romantic moment!

The idea for a botanic park came from two St. Albert citizens with a passion for horticulture: former mayor Richard Plain, and John Beedle, a retired city landscape planner. They wanted to publicly test and display tree, shrub, and perennial flower growth by planting a trial garden in the region's Zone 3 climate. This public garden in-progress is designed, planted, and maintained entirely by volunteers.

MORINVILLE

Directions: Travel north on St. Albert Trail, which becomes Hwy 2, and turn onto Hwy 642 east (Township Road 560).
Distance: 39.4 km, or about 38 minutes, from downtown Edmonton.
Info: The Morinville town office and information centre is located at 10125–100th Avenue. 780-939-4361; www.morinville.ca.

Morinville is named after Abbé Jean-Baptiste Morin (1852–1911). In 1890, Morin was asked to recruit Roman Catholic settlers from Quebec to the West. Under Monseigneur Grandin's supervision, he brought the first French settlers to the area from Quebec along with German settlers from the United States. Morinville was founded in spring 1891 with the arrival of almost 500 families, including the 43 adults who formed the parish.

The community opened a small post office in 1893 and grew quickly, due to its proximity to Edmonton and the discovery of coal in the area in 1895. Telephone lines connected Morinville to Edmonton in 1897, and two years later the first school opened. French culture exercised a strong influence over the town's development. In 1902 Father Ethier helped set up a French religious teaching order through a community of nuns called Les Filles de Jésus, or the Daughters of Jesus. The railway arrived in 1905, the same year Alberta became a province. Morinville went from colony to village status in 1908, and the following year became the third Alberta community to publish a newspaper.

Morinville incorporated as a town in 1911. In 1920 an extensive fire destroyed an entire business area on Main Street; however, many early buildings still stand as testament to Morinville's pioneer origins, and several have been declared official historic sites.

By 1967 Morinville's population exceeded 1,000; today it is home to almost 7,000 people. Immerse yourself in Morinville's fascinating multicultural history with a self-guided walking tour of the St. Jean Baptiste Church, the murals and monuments of Baptiste Park, and historical homes. Before starting out, obtain the Historical Walking

Baptiste Park in downtown Morinville

Tour Guide (revised 2008) at the Morinville town office and information centre. Ask about Morinville annual events, which include St. Jean Baptiste Day, Canada Day, Family Day, and Christmas festivities.

St. Jean Baptiste Church

Location: 10020–100th Avenue, Morinville.
Info: Interior viewing by appointment. 780-939-4816.

With its brick exterior, high steeple, and cross, the St. Jean Baptiste Church is Morinville's most beautiful landmark, but it is not its first place of worship. This church replaced a previous sanctuary here, located 3.3 kilometres west of the current townsite, which succeeded an 1891 log chapel built by Father St. Jean Baptiste.

Following a Quebec model, Father Arcade Ethier began building the St. Jean Baptiste Church in 1907. The parish used a $13,000 loan to fund construction but was left with a $1,200 debt, which proved an uncomfortable burden for the parishioners who celebrated their first mass here on January 1, 1908.

In 1916, the Stations of the Cross were installed—a series of 14 crosses that illustrate the stages of Jesus' final suffering, death, and burial. The church obtained its first harmonium, or reed organ, the following year, and in 1918 commissioned murals in the sanctuary (parishioners donated $50 each toward the painting). The church is known for its magnificent art, as well as its high, rounded ceiling.

A choir loft followed in 1925—the same year the Casavant pipe organ, built by the famous Casavant Frères company in St. Hyacinthe, Quebec, was installed. Blessed on November 7, 1926, the original four-bell carillon still chimes forth. Father A. Gauthier led the finishing of the church's interior, and in 1929 the brick exterior was added. Completely renovated in 1973, the church and rectory became Alberta's first officially designated historic site in 1974. A white 14-metre-high brick clock tower was built between the church and the rectory in 2005. Be sure to look for the medallion of Morin displayed inside the clock tower.

Next to St. Jean Baptiste Church, the Convent Notre Dame de la Visitation (10050–101st Street)—the Notre Dame Convent—was the Provincial House of the religious order of Les Filles de Jésus. This 4-storey, 100-room building was built in 1909, with the south and north wings added in 1920 and 1930, respectively. Today, the external structure of this provincial historic site is still the original, but the interior now holds residential apartments.

LEGAL

Directions: Exit Edmonton northbound on Hwy 28; turn left onto Secondary Hwy 803 (Range Road 243) and left again at Hwy 651 (Township Road 574).
Distance: 52 km, or about 46 minutes, from downtown Edmonton.
Info: Mural tours are available in French and English by phoning Ernie Chauvet at 780-910-1871 or 780-460-1034, or call L'Association canadienne-française de l'Alberta régionale Centralta (ACFA Centralta) at 1-866-KIOSQUE (546-7783).

The rolling landscape you pass on the way to Legal also welcomed the area's first settlers at the end of the 18th and beginning of the 19th centuries. Seeking the area's rich and fertile soil, most pioneers travelled from Quebec, but others arrived from Canada's eastern provinces, the United States, and Europe. Abbé Jean-Baptiste Morin, who founded Morinville, also recruited settlers from Quebec. Founded in 1891, the settlement was named after a man who spent many years as a missionary and became Edmonton's first Roman Catholic Archbishop: Monsignor Émile-Joseph Legal (1849–1920).

Legal's post office opened in May 1900. Over time, the community grew from a settlement into a village, and finally achieved status as a town on January 1, 1998. Two years later, official bilingual status was proclaimed. The area's strong cultural heritage and history is depicted in more than 28 murals located throughout the town. If you smell bread baking, follow your nose to the working open oven (*le four à pain*) found on Legal's 50th Street. During special events, summer visitors can taste the freshly baked bread made in the style of the area's pioneers.

THORHILD

Directions: Exit Edmonton on Manning Drive (Hwy 15) and turn left at 17 Street NE onto Hwy 28A. Continue on Hwy 28, turn left on Hwy 827, and turn left again to stay on Hwy 827 to Thorhild.
Distance: 85 km, or about 1 hour and 35 minutes, from Edmonton.
Info: 780-398-3688; www.thorhild.ca.

Thorhild is a farming community just 45 minutes northeast of Edmonton. Look for the Thorhild & District Museum in the village office complex (210–7th Avenue). It displays the heritage of Thorhild's Ukrainian, Polish, German, Slovak, and Finnish settlers, and also contains farming antiques, a prairie general store with everyday items, photos of original settlers, a Ukrainian wedding exhibit, and German and Slovak clothes. The museum is open to the public anytime the building is open—just ask someone at the village office to open the door. Admission is free.

Home to almost 500 people, Thorhild is called Alberta's Sunflower Village. Consider planning your trip for the last Sunday in August so you can witness the highly competitive Thorhild Sunflower Contest. This annual competition recognizes those who grow the tallest and smallest sunflower plants, and awards prizes for the largest sunflower head and the most flowers on one plant. While participants try to elevate their status in the sunflower-head throwing competition and seed-spitting contest, judges peruse sunflower arrangements and quilts, and search the village for the yard with the most creative sunflower theme.

REDWATER

Directions: Exit Edmonton on Manning Drive (Hwy 15) and turn left at 17 Street NE onto Hwy 28A. Continue on Hwy 28 and turn right at Hwy 38.
Distance: 62 km, or about 1 hour and 10 minutes, from Edmonton.
Info: 780-942-3519; www.town.redwater.ab.ca.

Redwater is named for its proximity to the Redwater River, a North Saskatchewan River tributary that gets its distinctive colour from nearby beds of ochre. Look for the Redwater & District Museum at 4916–48th Street, which reveals the lives of early pioneers and their experiences as the community grew from a hamlet to a town. The principal focus of the collection's approximately 10,000 objects is the early migration of people from various cultures, including Eastern European and Japanese immigrants. Admission is free. Hours fluctuate, but museum personnel will happily open by appointment. 780-942-3206.

WESTLOCK

Directions: Exit Edmonton on St. Albert Trail NW, and continue on Hwy 2. Turn left at Hwy 18.
Distance: 85 km, or about 1 hour and 12 minutes, from Edmonton.
Info: 1-866-349-4445; www.westlock.ca.

Home to just over 5,000 residents, the town of Westlock is located in the centre of one of Alberta's most prosperous mixed-farming areas. A survey once described this farmland as generating the highest yield for the lowest crop cost in North America.

Westlock is named after the land's original owners, the Westgate and Lockhart families, whose land was purchased for the current townsite in 1912 in preparation for the railway's arrival in 1913.

Canadian Tractor Museum

Location: South of Hwy 18 at 9704–96th Avenue, Westlock.
Info: Open from the Victoria Day weekend until the Labour Day weekend, Monday to Saturday, 11 a.m. to 4 p.m.; open at other times by appointment. 780-349-3353.

The Canadian Tractor Museum is home to the world's largest working weather vane. Perched atop a base more than 18.3 metres (60 feet) tall, a 1942 Case Model D tractor, with large, red, scalloped steel wheels, pivots as the 17.76-metre-long (55-foot) pointer follows the wind. Inside the museum you will find about 75 fully restored vintage tractors—models that are rotated from a collection of more than 200 units—including steam engines, a 1906 Sawyer Massey, and a functional 1916 Rumely.

Westlock Pioneer Museum and Visitor Information Centre

Location: 10216–100th Street, just off Hwy 18, Westlock.
Info: Open daily from Victoria Day to Labour Day, 10 a.m. to 5 p.m. Admission charged. Phone the Visitor Information Centre at 780-349-4849.

With more than 6,000 items displayed in different theme rooms, you will need some time to visit the Westlock Pioneer Museum. The Community Institutes Room includes school, hospital, and store artifacts. A pioneer kitchen displays authentic dishes, linens, and cookware, while the pioneer living room and bedroom are decorated with handmade quilts, stunning antique wedding gowns, and a full porcelain wash set originally from England. Be sure to look at the detailed displays that explain how pioneers did laundry and made butter. The Lamp Room contains a beautiful 140-piece Aladdin kerosene lamp collection, one of the largest of its kind in western Canada. You will also see a vast assortment of farming tools and equipment, along with a splendidly restored 1920 McLaughlin automobile. The Trueblood gun collection contains 95 guns and numerous types of ammunition. Browse or take a guided tour.

Edmonton Skydive Centre

Location: About 5 km east of Westlock. Exit Westlock eastbound. After 4 km, turn left into the airport at the Westlock Airport sign and follow the road to the end.
Info: 780-444-JUMP (5867); www.edmontonskydive.com.

The Edmonton Skydive Centre offers instruction and coaching for both recreational jumpers and those aiming to become professional skydivers. Jumping depends on the weather, so if it's raining, snowing, or colder than minus 10 Celsius, planes won't take off. Winds faster than 24 km per hour and low cloud cover can also stall skydiving activities. If this happens, just visit the centre's No Pull Café and chat up some jumpers while you wait for the weather to change!

WESTLOCK PICNIC AREAS

If you bring a picnic, consider unpacking it at the scenic **Lindahl Park** next to the Westlock Pioneer Museum. Also nearby is the **Mountie Park Recreation Area**, at 100th Street and 96th Avenue, which has a playground, horseshoe pits, tennis courts, and ball diamonds. Rotary Trail loops into natural areas with pathways for walking, jogging, inline skating, and cycling.

Other picnic areas include **Rainbow Park**, a day-use area about 6.5 kilometres east, then 1.5 kilometres south of Westlock on Highway 18. Located 38.6 kilometres north of Westlock, **Long Island Lake Municipal Park** is ideal for those who wish to boat, fish, or swim. To reach the park, located on about 57 hectares (140 acres) at the north end of the lake, travel 22 kilometres north from Westlock on Highway 44 to Dapp Corner (turn right at the store), continue 12 kilometres north on Highway 801, then turn right to travel 3 kilometres east.

BARRHEAD

Directions: Exit Edmonton on Hwy 16 west, turn right onto Hwy 43 north, and right at Hwy 33.
Distance: 121 km, or about 1 hour and 30 minutes, from downtown Edmonton.
Info: 780-674-3301; www.barrhead.ca.

Nestled in the valley of the Paddle River, Barrhead is situated on the southern edge of the boreal forest. Settlers began coming to the valley in 1906, mostly from Britain and the United States. They set up sawmills to take advantage of the extensive timber and cleared land to grow cereal crops, but the community's location near the now-historic Klondike Trail is what helped the town grow as a trade centre. Hundreds of gold seekers passed through during the Klondike Gold Rush, triggered by the 1896 discovery of gold in Bonanza Creek, Yukon. The town of Barrhead is also near the historic fur-trade trail that linked Edmonton and Fort Assiniboine.

Incorporated as a town in 1946, Barrhead was named after the birthplace of an early settler—James McGuire from Barrhead in East Renfrewshire, Scotland. In January 1914, a post office was opened, and the community began to settle around it and other establishments, such as the community hall and store run by the Paddle River and District Co-operative Society. The town, originally located 3.25 kilometres to the northwest, moved to its current location in 1927 when the Pembina Valley Railway arrived.

A town with an agricultural base, and a population of 4,209 at last count, Barrhead is a popular launching spot for outdoor enthusiasts seeking lakes and wilderness. Barrhead County features three rivers, numerous lakes, and the Natural Sandhills Ecological Area. Watch for the town mascot—Aaron the blue heron—near the large gazebo in Barrhead's town centre. For a beautiful trek in any season, travel the Blue Heron Trail, which winds through various town parks and includes a boardwalk along the picturesque Paddle River. Start at 48th Avenue and 50th Street, next to the Paddle River Golf Course's ninth hole. Walkways follow the Paddle River from the Paddle Golf Course through Beaver Brook to Barrhead Golf and Recreation Area. It is groomed for cross-country skiing in the winter. (780-674-2532.)

Some of Barrhead's annual events include an Ice Carnival in March, Blue Heron Fair Days in August, Volksmarch in June, and the Wildrose Rodeo Finals and Centre of Alberta Volksmarch in September.

Barrhead picnic spots include Clear Lake (780-674-5307), Elks Beach on Lac La Nonne (780-967-5029), and Peanut Lake (780-674-3331).

Barrhead & District Centennial Museum and Barrhead Visitor Information Centre

Location: 5629–49th Street, three blocks north of Barrhead on Hwy 33.
Info: Open Tuesday to Saturday from 10 a.m. to 5 p.m. Barrhead Visitor Information Centre open from May through September. 780-674-5203.

The Barrhead Centennial Museum contains an astonishing array of artifacts that reveal how early settlers coped with daily life. The collection includes farm equipment, pioneer furniture, and an especially interesting map that details the route of the Klondike Trail through the County of Barrhead. You can also see the third-largest privately owned exhibit of African artifacts in Canada, as well as a collection of the local newspaper archive dating back to 1928.

Thunder Lake Provincial Park

Location: 18 km west of Barrhead on Hwy 18 (Township Road 594).
Info: 780-674-4051.

Thunder Lake Provincial Park is a favourite for those who love to go out in a boat or swim from a sandy beach. In addition to trails for hiking and cycling, the park offers a wide assortment of possible activities, including bird-watching, fishing, powerboating, sailing, volleyball, water-skiing, windsurfing, and baseball. You will find change rooms, a boat ramp, a pier, fish-cleaning stations, a playground, and a summertime store. Winter visitors can cross-country ski on park trails, and ice fishing is also an option.

Klondike Ferry Crossing

Location: 42 km, or about 40 minutes, from Barrhead. Exit Barrhead on Hwy 33 north, turn right at Hwy 16. Travel 1.6 km and then turn left at Hwy 769 (8 km west of Vega along Hwy 661).
Info: The ferry operates from April though October, and an ice bridge is available for winter crossing. 780-674-3331.

One of only seven remaining ferries in Alberta, the cabled Klondike Ferry near Vega crosses the Athabasca River into the Fort Assiniboine Sandhills Wildland Provincial Park—an area with many hiking and cycling trails to explore. A conserved natural and historic area, Klondike Ferry Park is a nice place to stop for a picnic and a scenic walk or bike ride. A sheltered cooking site is available, as are outdoor toilets.

WESTLOCK–BARRHEAD LOOP

Westlock and Barrhead are 41.7 kilometres, or about 34 minutes, apart. The first stop is the growing agricultural community of Westlock, with museums, parks, and the Edmonton Skydive Centre, where you may well see parachutists in action. The Barrhead portion of the loop takes you near the historic Klondike Trail, and to sand dunes and one of the few ferries on the prairies.

Exit Westlock on Hwy 18. Turn left at the Hwy 33 junction to remain on Hwy 18 to Barrhead.

FORT ASSINIBOINE

Directions: From Edmonton, take Hwy 16 west, exit onto Hwy 43 north, turn left at Hwy 33 toward Barrhead, turn right at Hwy 661, and follow to Fort Assiniboine.
Distance: 161 km, or 2 hours and 19 minutes, from Edmonton.
Info: 780-778-8400; 1-888-870-6315; www.woodlands.ab.ca.

Records spanning the Hudson's Bay era (1823–1877) show that Fort Assiniboine served as a supply point for settlers. Later, stampeders making the long trek to the Klondike followed a northwest path from Edmonton to Dawson City in Yukon Territory, with gold seekers wintering at Klondike City, about 16 kilometres north of Fort Assiniboine, in 1898 and 1899. During the gold rush, the North-West Territories government sent T. W. Chalmers to make a trail from Klondike City to Lesser Slave Lake, in central Alberta. The Canadian government, as well as Edmontonians, promoted the trail as the all-Canadian route to the easy gold of the Yukon.

A group of Fort Assiniboine residents formed the Klondike Trail Society to recognize Chalmers's section of the trail. They are working to locate, map, and mark the first 250 miles leading out of Edmonton to Dawson City—the section of the Klondike Trail now called Grizzly Trail Highway 33. Most of the stampeders who attempted this treacherous route to the Yukon arrived too late to stake claims. Others gave up before reaching the goldfields and settled in Fort Assiniboine and other communities as they headed north.

In 2005, Fort Assiniboine became home to the world's largest wagon wheel and pickaxe. Next to the Fort Assiniboine Museum, the 7.3-metre-tall (24 foot) wheel and 6-metre-tall (20 foot) pickaxe commemorate the pioneers who built the community of Fort Assiniboine, the gold seekers who camped in the area, and the community's place as home to Alberta's second-oldest fort.

Fort Assiniboine

Annual Fort Assiniboine events include the Hamlet Hoedown, as well as a dramatic re-enactment of the night Jesus was born called Journey to Bethlehem, which is held during the last two weekends of November.

Fort Assiniboine Museum

Location: On State Avenue in Fort Assiniboine, at the wagon wheel and pickaxe.
Info: Open noon to 5 p.m. 780-584-3737.

Fort Assiniboine's history is commemorated in a museum constructed in the style of the Hudson's Bay Fort that was located here during the Klondike Gold Rush. The museum portrays Klondike history and contains pioneer furniture, tools, traps, farm equipment, some of the nails from the original fort, wildlife exhibits, and a schoolhouse.

Fort Assiniboine Sandhills Wildland Provincial Park

Location: The Central and viewpoint staging areas are 30 km north of Fort Assiniboine on Hwy 661; the Klondike staging area is about 15 km north.
Info: 780-960-8170 or Parks Division Headquarters at 1-866-427-3582; or 780-427-3582.

Fort Assiniboine Sandhills Wildland is a remote backcountry provincial park in the boreal forest, located along the north shore of the Athabasca River. You will see a wide range of landscapes here, including steep valley walls, river flats, springs, wetlands, and stable sand dunes, as well as pine, white spruce, and aspen forests. The park is an outdoor enthusiast's delight, with opportunities for birding, fishing, backcountry hiking, and wildlife watching. It is also a worthwhile location in which to seek and identify wildflowers, as more than 435 plant species have been documented here. Visit the interpretive viewpoint to see the Athabasca River and surrounding landscape. The park has three day-use sites: Central Staging Area, Athabasca Viewpoint Staging Area, and Klondike Trail Staging Area. Follow the trail signs to hike part of the Klondike Trail used by gold

Wagon wheel and pickaxe next to the Fort Assiniboine Museum

seekers who flocked northward to the goldfields. The staging areas have small parking lots, and the Klondike and Viewpoint staging areas each have a picnic table.

Holmes Crossing Sandhills Ecological Reserve and Holmes Crossing Recreation Area

Location: About 4 km southwest of Fort Assiniboine on Hwy 33; the reserve and recreation area border are on the south bank of the Athabasca River.
Info: Holmes Crossing is available for foot traffic only; equestrian use is prohibited. County of Barrhead: 780-674-3331.

Sand dunes cover about 26,000 square kilometres, or 0.27 percent, of Canada's total area and 45 percent of those dunes are in Alberta. Chinook winds blowing from the mountains concentrate most of the dunes in the west of the province, on the open prairie. Stable sand dunes, low-lying wetlands, and rolling landscape define the Holmes Crossing Sandhills Ecological Reserve, an especially beautiful area

along the Athabasca River valley. White spruce, aspen, and balsam poplar dominate the comparatively moist river valley, while jack pine and aspen grow in pure stands or mixed-wood forests on the dunes. The reserve contains one of Canada's few examples of transverse dunes—the result of abundant sediment and wind patterns that maintain the same general direction.

In this fantastic area for observing wildlife, you may spot deer and moose, especially along the river valley. Pay special attention to signs of bears in the area, and be sure to practise bear safety. Birds are plentiful, with the common nighthawk, solitary vireo, pine siskin, and purple finch frequenting the pinewoods. Also watch for the less frequently seen great grey owl, Cooper's hawk, pileated woodpecker, and sandhill crane.

Encompassing 1,983 hectares (4,899 acres), the reserve is a diverse and interesting site, providing opportunities for hiking, wildlife viewing, picnicking, fishing, canoeing, kayaking, horseback riding, and gold panning. Next to the reserve, the Holmes Crossing Recreation Area has sheltered picnic sites, outdoor toilets, walking trails to springs, and a cooking shelter with a heating stove, which a creative cook could use to prepare a meal. Fun to visit in any season, you can cross-country ski, snowshoe, and snowmobile here in winter.

ATHABASCA

Directions: Exit Edmonton on Hwy 2 north, bear right at Hwy 18 east, which is also Hwy 2, and continue north to Athabasca.
Distance: 152 km, or about 2 hours, from Edmonton.
Info: Athabasca Country Tourism: 1-877-211-8669; www.athabascacountry.com.

An alternative, more scenic route to Athabasca is along the old highway—a well-maintained gravel road. Although not currently signed as a different course, you can access this north–south road from Tawatinaw, Rochester, Perryvale, and Colinton. Be sure to watch for birds near the numerous bluebird boxes along the way. You might want to visit Perryvale's traditional general store, as well as its two classic-style churches, charming picnic grounds, and apiary. Nestled in a stunning valley, the hamlet of Colinton has a number of stores and cafés, including the historic Colinton Hotel.

One of North America's longest undammed rivers, the Athabasca River flows 1,231 kilometres from the Rocky Mountains to Lake Athabasca; it eventually reaches the Arctic Ocean via the Mackenzie River system. Flowing through the town of Athabasca (formerly Athabasca Landing), it is a reminder of the historic days when scows and paddlewheel steamers travelled the river in the late 19th and early 20th centuries.

Athabasca Landing was a significant trade link between the prairies and distant northwest from 1876 to 1913. It became the main transfer spot for all goods sent north and for all furs shipped south using the Athabasca, Peace, and Mackenzie River systems. Missionaries followed the fur traders, with Anglicans arriving first in 1884 and

Rotary Trail on the Athabasca riverfront

ATHABASCA COUNTRY TOURISM

making the Landing the centre of their missionary operations. Roman Catholics and Methodists followed, and the North West Mounted Police arrived by 1893.

> "This is the Law of the Yukon, that only the Strong shall thrive; That surely the Weak shall perish, and only the Fit survive." —Robert Service

In 1898, about 600 prospectors used the Athabasca Landing Trail on their way north, either crossing the river and travelling up river by boat or going west on the Peace River Trail. Poet Robert W. Service, famous for his poems about the Yukon frontier and gold seekers, is believed to have enlisted to serve in World War I in Athabasca and to have worked at the Imperial Bank. *The Shooting of Dan McGrew* and *The Cremation of Sam McGee* are known around the world.

Athabasca Landing grew as the centre of the northern transportation system, but its significance ended when the railway failed to expand northeast and northwest from the town. The community became an incorporated town called Athabasca Landing in 1911, with "Landing" dropped from the name in 1913. The name Athabasca is believed to have come from the Cree *athapaskaw* and means "where there are reeds or grass." Athabasca and the surrounding area offer Northern Alberta wilderness recreation, heritage experiences, industrial tours, and the chance to learn how to steer a dogsled. Summer daylight hours are even slightly longer than in Edmonton, meaning more daylight hours to enjoy the region.

The population of Athabasca is 2,575. For a great view of the community, visit the scenic Centennial Park Lookout on the side of the river opposite the town. Follow Highway 813 north and take the first left after the bridge. Keep to the left route going up the hill, and follow the signs to the nearby lookout.

A pleasant way to get a feel for Athabasca is to walk around town, aided by historic signage that reveals the community's history. You can get a walking heritage tour map from the tourist information

centre, the Alice B. Donahue Library, or from www.town.athabasca
.ab.ca. The tour will take you past the Athabasca Train Station, Old
Brick School, Athabasca United Church, and Grand Union Hotel,
which has been serving the community since 1914. During World
War II, seemingly endless US convoys passed through Athabasca as
they travelled Highway 2—once called the Alcan Highway—to access
Alaska via the Alaska Highway at Dawson Creek. US truckers boarded
at the always-full Union Hotel, sometimes with men using sleeping
bags that they laid out in the lobby. The truckers were forced to leave
their diesel trucks running all night when temperatures dipped to
minus 50–60 degrees Fahrenheit, and on those days local residents
woke to a haze of blue smoke over the town.

Just off Highway 2 west on University Drive is Athabasca University, Canada's largest online and distance education provider. It offers
more than 700 courses for about 37,000 students in at least 87 countries. Ask for a free tour to see its facilities, art collection, and library.
To book a tour in advance, call 1-866-788-9041, ext. 6109; go to www
.athabascau.ca for more information.

Tourist Information Caboose and Rotary Riverfront Trail

Location: 50th Avenue and 47th Street, Athabasca.
Info: 1-877-211-8669.

Look for the tourist information centre, which is housed in a distinctive Canadian National Railways caboose on the Athabasca riverfront.
Summertime visitors who would like to arrange for a guided walking Heritage Tour of (or around) the town's historic buildings must
make arrangements ahead of time by calling the Athabasca Country
Tourism Coordinator at the phone number above. If you prefer a
self-guided tour, pick up a booklet about historic houses from the
Tourist Information Caboose, Alice B. Donahue Library and Archives,
or town office.

The Tawatinaw Creek enters the Athabasca River at the campground
adjacent to the tourist information centre caboose. You can walk the

ATHABASCA COUNTY TOURISM

Muskeg Creek

Rotary Riverfront Trail and read interpretive signs that explain early transportation, boat building, river trackers, area settlers, natural history, and commerce at Athabasca Landing. Murals on Athabasca's riverfront buildings depict scenes of the days when trappers, as well as Cree and Métis river trackers ruled the river. A short walk up 48th Street reveals a mural that honours Athabascans who have served in the Canadian Forces.

Muskeg Creek Trails

Location: The trailhead borders Landing Trail Intermediate School at 5502–48th Avenue, Athabasca.

Info: Neither motorized vehicles nor pets are allowed on the trail. Contact Athabasca Regional Recreation for maps or to borrow a key for the log chalet. 780-675-2967.

Those who embrace the outdoors in all seasons will also appreciate the trails in Muskeg Creek Valley—an Athabascan treasure. The

Muskeg Creek Trail system has 17.5 kilometres of trails, accessible right from town. In winter, the hilly terrain is groomed for cross-country skiers and provides both Nordic and skate skiers with a pleasant challenge. Those who prefer to snowshoe will also enjoy exploring these pathways. The 1.5-kilometre trail is lit for nighttime users. Maps are posted along the trail, and outhouses and a chalet with a wood-burning stove are available. The trail connects to the Rotary Riverfront Trail, as well as to Athabasca University.

Meanook Biological Research Station

Location: 13.7 km, or about 13 minutes, south of Athabasca on Hwy 2. Turn right at Township Road 652.
Info: Tours are available during the field season, which runs from May through September. All tours must be booked in advance. 780-675-4934.

The Cree named this area *Meanook,* which means "a good camping place." A University of Alberta, Faculty of Science research facility, the Meanook Biological Research Station is located on a 214-hectare National Wildlife Area (NWA) in the boreal forest and aspen parkland transition zone. With its easy access to continuous and fragmented mixed-wood boreal forest, peatlands, wetlands, agricultural land, and a wide variety of lakes, rivers, and creeks, there are no similar facilities on the western plains. Visitors are welcome to tour the field sites and laboratories where scientists research terrestrial and aquatic species. It's also worth checking out the meteorological station and experimental ponds. Open year-round, the research station provides a great opportunity to watch scientists on the job.

Amber Valley Community Cultural Centre and Obadiah Place

Location: About 18 km, about 15 minutes, east of Athabasca on Hwy 55. Follow the blue and white provincial signs to the Amber Valley Community Cultural Centre. Note that there is no signage to Obadiah Place.
Info: Open by appointment on Saturdays in July and August. Guided tours are available. 780-675-2230; www.athabascacountry.com (go to "Heritage").

Mrs. Willie Kinamore (left) with her mother-in-law, Henrietta Kinamore, circa 1909, at Amber Valley

Originally named Pine Creek, the community of Amber Valley comprised Alberta's largest group of African-Canadian settlers, some of whom came from Oklahoma in 1911 to avoid repressive laws that forbade them from voting and restricted their liberties. They rented boxcars and travelled with livestock and all their possessions, passing through Edmonton to Athabasca Landing. Here they faced 32 kilometres of tedious travel through muskeg and deep forest. Harsh winters, crop failures, and the struggles of clearing treed land made the first few years extremely challenging. A school was opened in 1913 and a non-denominational church the following year.

The Amber Valley Community Cultural Centre has an important place in the community's history and has a museum attached. A designated provincial historic resource, Obadiah Place is an Amber Valley homestead that is being converted into a museum. It is named for Obadiah Bowen, who grew up in the house and lived in Amber Valley until 1996. From the Amber Valley Community Cultural Centre, Obadiah Place is 3.2 kilometres (2 miles) farther east on Highway 55: turn south onto Amber Valley Road and watch for the homestead on the east side.

Athabasca Landing Trail

Location: Look for the trailhead at the end of 45th Street (the first southbound street after the bridge that crosses the Tawatinaw River) in Athabasca.
Info: Snowmobiles and all-terrain vehicles are not allowed.

In 1876, Athabasca Landing Trail was the first overland route between Edmonton and Athabasca Landing. The Hudson's Bay Company established the trail to improve and expand northern transportation. It linked the North Saskatchewan River with the Mackenzie River system and became Canada's busiest northern route for 40 years. As the railway expanded, the trail became less important. The path that remains from this historic course begins at Gibbons and ends in Athabasca. It is part of the Trans Canada Trail, the longest trail in the world.

The Athabasca–Perryvale portion of the trail is 32 kilometres. Its surface is natural in parts, with some corduroy, gravel, and dirt surfaces, so you can expect some soggy, boggy parts in spring. The trail may be used for hiking, cycling, Nordic skiing, horseback riding, snowshoeing, and dogsledding. Trailheads are marked in Athabasca, Colinton, and Perryvale. The trail follows the Old Landing Trail most

Baptiste Lake day-use area

closely between Perryvale and Meanook. A Trans Canada Trail pavilion is located at the Athabasca trailhead.

While beyond the two-hour day-trip range of this book, hikers of historic trails will be interested to know that the Klondike–Peace River Trail begins 30 kilometres north of Athabasca (take Highway 813 north from Athabasca, and turn left at the Sawdy turnoff). The Old Peace River Trail enabled early Aboriginals, trappers, and gold seekers to continue the route north. The trail contains historical points of interest, including gravesites and the Tomato Creek stopping house.

Baptiste Lake

Location: 18.6 km, or about 16 minutes, west of Athabasca on Hwy 2; at the intersection where Hwy 2 turns north, continue straight on Township Road 663A and follow this road until you see the park.
Info: 780-675-2273; www.athabascacounty.com (go to "Parks & Recreation").

A group of Métis from Saskatchewan settled in long, narrow lake-front lots along Baptiste Lake in the 1880s. Farming began in 1904, and by 1909 the land that remained was offered to homesteaders. Much of the agricultural land you see around this lake was broken before 1915. Baptiste Lake is named after an early settler: Baptiste Majeau.

The Athabasca County day-use area located on the southwest corner of Baptiste Lake provides a boat launch, large dock, washrooms, change rooms, picnic shelter, tables, and playground. There is a concession across the road at a private campground. Although sometimes susceptible to blue-green algae, the lake is used extensively for swimming and boating, as well as for fishing for yellow perch, northern pike, and walleye. Narrows connect two lake basins—the shallower northern basin is up to 16 metres deep, while the southern basin descends 28 metres.

Forfar Recreation Park

Location: 18 km south of Athabasca on Hwy 2, and then 23 km west on Hwy 663.
Info: 780-675-2273; www.athabascacounty.com (go to "Parks & Recreation").

Located on a different Long Lake than the one near Boyle (see Long Lake Provincial Park, page 46), Forfar Recreation Park has two very nice beach areas, a boat launch, picnic tables, firepits (with firewood available), a playground, and walking trails. There is a small day-use charge per vehicle.

BOYLE

Directions: Exit Edmonton on Hwy 28A east; turn left at Hwy 831.
Distance: 149 km, or about 1 hour and 56 minutes, from Edmonton.
Info: 780-689-3643; www.boylealberta.com.

The village of Boyle was named to commemorate a man who gave much of his life to public service. John Robert Boyle wanted to become

a lawyer but could not afford to further his education. He taught school until he had saved up enough to return to his studies and was admitted to the bar in 1899. Boyle went on to become Alberta's minister of education in 1913 and a member of Canada's Supreme Court in 1924. He held the latter position until his death in 1936. His name also marks the Edmonton Boyle Street neighbourhood.

Home to 840 people, the village of Boyle is near the centre of numerous outdoor recreation sites, including nearby Long Lake Provincial Park, Skeleton Lake, and North Buck Lake. Flat Lake is popular for birding, and Hope Lake for picking blueberries. Hope Lake Campground, 20 kilometres northeast of Boyle, off Highway 63, has a nice sandy beach, as well as a playground, boat launch, and private boat rentals. There is a 12-kilometres-per-hour boat-speed limit, and a $4 day-use fee per vehicle.

Long Lake Provincial Park

Location: 20 km south of Boyle on Secondary Hwy 831, and then 2 km northeast on the access road.
Info: 780-675-8213.

Long Lake Provincial Park is part of a scenic glacial meltwater channel, covered with mixed-wood boreal forest. This long, winding lake and popular park is a great place to launch a canoe or kayak, swim, or play horseshoes. Visitors come to fish, hike, mountain bike, use powerboats, water ski, sail, and windsurf. You will find a boat ramp, boat rentals, hand launch, change rooms, fish-cleaning stations, pier, pit and flush toilets, picnic shelters with and without stoves, a concession, and a grocery store. Winter visitors can ice-fish and use the 12 kilometres of ungroomed cross-country ski trails. A warm-up shelter is available.

Alberta Pacific Forestry Industries (Al-Pac)

Location: About 40 km northwest of Boyle. Take Hwy 63 north, turn west on Hwy 55, and then right onto Hwy 63—the Alberta Pacific Connector Road.

Info: Tours are available from May through August. Due to safety considerations, participants must be 12 years of age or older. Admission is free. Call ahead to confirm dates and times. 780-525-8000 or 1-800-661-5210; www.alpac.ca (go to "Community").

One of the most modern pulp mills in the world, Alberta-Pacific Forest Industries Inc. (Al-Pac) annually produces about 650,000 tons of high-quality, elemental-chlorine-free bleached kraft pulp. Using mostly deciduous trees, such as trembling aspen and balsam poplar, Al-Pac is licensed to sustainably harvest an area in northeastern Alberta that encompasses 5.8 million hectares—a region roughly the size of Nova Scotia. About two million hectares of this area are harvestable.

You can take an indoor and outdoor tour of the facility. The indoor tour shows how trees are made into pulp and how the pulp is bleached. You will see the control room and the chemical recovery and utilities areas where power is generated from steam and chemicals are recycled. The tour also visits the machine room where pulp is made into sheets which are then cut and baled.

The outdoor excursion views the giant Portal Kranco cranes moving logs from trucks to the log pile. Visitors pass the wood room, where logs are stripped, chipped, and sprayed into piles to age before entering the pulping process. A trip to the Water and Effluent Treatment area, known on-site as the Bug Farm, shows how microscopic creatures reduce mill waste.

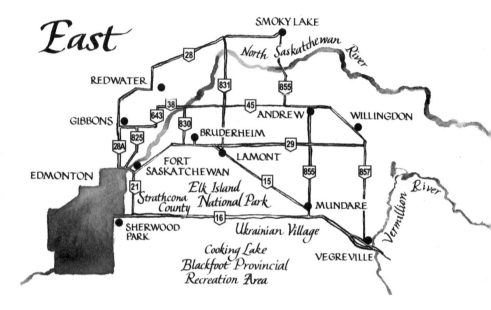

EAST OF EDMONTON

East-central Alberta visitors enter the heritage district known as the Kalyna (pronounced *kah-LEHN-ah*) Country Ecomuseum, a multicultural area where visitors can see historical attractions in their original settings. *Kalyna* is a Slavic term for "high bush cranberry." The Ukrainian Cultural Heritage Village is one Kalyna Country destination that can easily take up the better part of a day. Interacting with the costumed interpreters at this open-air museum will make you feel like a time traveller.

Just 3 kilometres from here is the entrance, via the highway, to the only national park within a short drive of Edmonton. Elk Island National Park has a far-reaching natural and cultural heritage that includes spectacular views, self-guided trails, floating boardwalks, and historic buildings. Part of the dark sky network, the park has set aside an area that is devoid of light to increase night sky visibility. In addition to improving conditions for astronomy aficionados, the dark sky preserve benefits plants and animals that require uninterrupted nocturnal conditions to survive and thrive.

The parkland region falls between the dense mixed-wood boreal forest to the north and prairie grassland to the south. East of Edmonton, the parkland features many areas where birds and other animals enjoy shelter and abundant food supplies in natural settings. There are also places where visitors can enjoy wildlife watching and other outdoor recreation opportunities. Trembling aspen and balsam poplar are common, favouring richer soils where fires have occurred.

SIMPLE SUMMER FAMILY DAY TRIP
Total driving time: about 3 hours

When heading east, make your first stop at Sherwood Park's **Strathcona County Museum & Archives** (page 53). Enjoy a fun lunch at the train cars at **Katie's Crossing** (page 55) in Ardrossan, then head to Fort Saskatchewan to take pictures with the city's lawn-mowing sheep. Choose to either visit the **Fort Saskatchewan Museum and Historic Site** (page 64) or the **Stratotech Park International Raceway** (page 65). Make sure to check the race schedule before you leave home.

From Fort Saskatchewan, travel to Mundare to take a tour of the sausage-making operation at **Stawnichy's Meat Processing** (page 75). Purchase some fresh sausage to add to your suppertime picnic and plan to see the internationally renowned Mundare Ukrainian Sausage statue before driving to **Elk Island National Park** (page 56) to explore and relax over a suppertime picnic. National park fees do apply at Elk Island, so depending on time and budget, you may want to save this park for a full day excursion and picnic at the **Cooking Lake–Blackfoot Provincial Recreation Area** (page 59).

Watch for old farmhouses and barns, often standing alone in the middle of a field, or surrounded by a windbreak of mature trees. Sometimes near collapse, many of these picturesque buildings date back to the late 19th century.

Smeltzer House in Sherwood Park is an example of 1920s brick architecture, and the Strathcona County Museum & Archives displays articles that early homesteaders made and used.

This region has become the land of giant statues, including the Vegreville Easter egg, the Mundare sausage, and Andrew's mallard duck. Also unique in the area is Fort Saskatchewan's live lawn mowers, a flock of sheep guided by a shepherd who ensures city grass is shorn to an appropriate level.

Central Rural East Alberta Museums offer pioneer heritage displays, artifacts, demonstrations, and events. The Lamont County Church Tour reveals stunning architecture and provides a glimpse into the spirituality that continues to sustain church members.

SHERWOOD PARK

Directions: Exit Edmonton on Hwy 16 east.
Distance: 22.5 km, or about 24 minutes, from Edmonton.
Info: www.strathconacounty.com.

Directly east of Edmonton, and part of Strathcona County, Sherwood Park is sometimes called the world's largest hamlet, with its population of 56,845 residents. Despite its size, the community remains a hamlet because urban centres in Alberta are defined by the way they are administered rather than by population or geographic size. The Alberta government granted Strathcona County status as a specialized municipality—with funding options under both urban and rural frameworks. Strathcona County is also noteworthy for being the first rural area to become self-governing when Alberta was still part of the Northwest Territories.

A statue of the Lendrum sisters, some of the original settlers in the area.

Sherwood Park formed in 1952 as a result of the efforts of John Hook Campbell and John Mitchell, who wanted to establish a satellite community for the many new workers who came to find jobs in the oil industry. Strathcona's Municipal Council approved the idea in 1953, and the first residents arrived in the winter of 1955–56. Glen MacLachlan opened the first food store and coffee shop on the corner of what is now Alder Avenue and Hawthorne Street.

In 1956, Canada Post refused Campbelltown and Campbell Park as possible names for the community, but accepted Sherwood Park. The inspiration for the name is unknown, but is thought to have been chosen simply as an appropriate description for homes set in a rural area.

You can get a feel for what Strathcona County was like in the early 20th century, before Sherwood Park existed, by walking the Heritage Mile. Start at the path alongside the Broadmoor Boulevard traffic circle and walk toward Main Boulevard: Smeltzer House, the Lendrum Sisters sculpture, and Salisbury United Church lie on the east side of the boulevard; the Ottewell Centre house and barn, Monument Park, and historic Smyth Farm populate the west side of the road. *Journey Back in Time,* a 100-page guide, is sold at the Strathcona County Museum & Archives.

Strathcona County Museum & Archives

Location: 913 Ash Street, Sherwood Park.
Info: Open Monday to Friday, 10 a.m. to 4 p.m. Admission charged. 780-467-8189; www.strathconacountymuseum.ca; strathconacountymuseum@shaw.ca.

The Strathcona County Museum & Archives is located in the building that housed Sherwood Park's original fire hall in 1959, as well as the first RCMP station in 1967.

Today the building exhibits artifacts from the lives of Aboriginal people and area settlers of the early 1900s. This is a museum in which you really get a genuine impression of pioneer life. You will find a train station, grain elevator, dairy barn, blacksmith/woodworking shop, general store/post office, barbershop, parlour, kitchen, one-room school, country church, jail cell, and other displays. Be sure to notice the homemade wooden shovel and rake as you enter the museum. Call and book a tour to be led by a costumed interpreter, or explore the many well-organized exhibits independently.

Smeltzer House

Location: 1 Broadmoor Boulevard, Sherwood Park.
Info: 780-464-2023.

Built in 1920, Smeltzer House was the home of Maurice Smeltzer and his wife, Eliza Pithie, a descendant of the Scottish poet Robert Burns. Originally from Ontario, Smeltzer delivered workhorses to Edmonton and then settled on a 194-hectare (480 acre) homestead in the Salisbury area in 1892. His brother-in-law Cyril Fry designed the Canadian four-square-style house, which was adopted as a common model of construction in the early 1900s. The house stands on brick footings and has two solid brick walls separated by an air space. A historic resource, Smeltzer House became a visual arts centre in 1985 that offers a variety of creative and unique visual arts and pottery programs throughout the year. The original 1930s garage contains the Clay Hut Pottery Studio.

Sherwood Park Natural Area

Location: About 4 km south of Wye Road. From Wye Road, turn south on Range Road 231.

The Sherwood Park Natural Area offers year-round hiking on 3 kilometres of developed trails. The historic bonus is that you will be traipsing the path of a wagon track used in the early 1900s by people travelling between Edmonton and Cooking Lake. The old Edmonton Trail passes through rolling landscape with wetland areas and a large slough. The mosaic of habitats here draws a number of bird species, including hairy and downy woodpeckers, great horned owls, and petite northern saw-whet owls.

Strathcona Wilderness Centre

Location: 16 km east of Sherwood Park on Baseline Road (Township Road 530), and turn south on Range Road 212.
Info: Open daily 9 a.m. to 4:30 p.m. Wheelchair accessible. 780-922-3939, or for 24-hour information call 780-467-5800, ext. 371; www.strathcona.ab.ca/wilder nesscentre; swcinfo@strathcona.ab.ca.

Encompassing 223 hectares (550 acres) of parkland, the Strathcona Wilderness Centre offers year-round nature exploration on the shores of Bennett Lake. Stop at the information centre to ask about picnic sites and current conditions of the 12 kilometres of trails, including 3 kilometres of interpretive pathways. There is a spruce bog boardwalk to explore, and you can rent a canoe when water levels are high enough. Snowshoes and cross-country skis are available for rent in the winter.

Katie's Crossing, Ardrossan

Location: Just east of Sherwood Park; go east along Baseline Road, and cross Range Road 222. Katie's Crossing is on the right-hand side at the junction of Range Road 221A and Baseline Road—before the train trestle.
Info: Open year-round, usually 12 p.m. to 8 p.m. on Thursday, Friday, and Saturday, and 12 p.m. to 7 p.m. on Sunday. Cash only. Limited wheelchair access. Call ahead for hours or tour information. 780-922-7008.

Katie's Crossing is a restaurant located in vintage railway cars. You can dine inside one of the railway cars or take your food to the outside deck or a picnic table during the summer months. Explore the train while your hobo bologna sandwich is prepared. One of the train cars has been made into a chapel, and another contains a collection of antiques, with some items for sale. Call about a week ahead if you would like a guided tour of all ten train cars.

Ukrainian Cultural Heritage Village

Location: 35 km east of Sherwood Park on Hwy 16.
Info: From Victoria Day weekend to Labour Day weekend, open 10 a.m. to 6 p.m.; and until Thanksgiving, from 10 a.m. to 4 p.m. Open for special events throughout the rest of the year. To avoid disturbing horses and livestock, please leave pets at home. Those travelling with pets must leave them in the main visitor parking area. Call toll-free (from within Alberta only) 310-0000, then dial 780-662-3640.

The Ukrainian Cultural Heritage Village depicts Ukrainian settlement in east-central Alberta from 1892 to 1930 and portrays the struggles early pioneers faced as they turned forest into farmland. The village is a fascinating place to explore with more than 30 restored buildings, costumed interpreters, wagon rides, and farm animals. The taste of fresh bread baked daily in a clay oven will make you feel you have arrived in a thriving community. You will find farmsteads, three Eastern Byzantine churches, a fully functioning grain elevator, a blacksmith shop, a sod hut, and a townsite. A plethora of special events

Field of historic Red Fife wheat at the Ukrainian Cultural Heritage Village

are held each summer at this multiple-award-winning provincial historic site.

ELK ISLAND NATIONAL PARK

Distance: 48 km east of Edmonton on Hwy 16.
Info: Open every day of the year. Entry and service fees are listed on the website: www.pc.gc.ca/pn-np/ab/elkisland. Note: swimming is not recommended.

Located in the Beaver Hills, Elk Island National Park is unique because of its aspen thickets surrounding prairie. Because so much land has been acquired for farmland and community development, aspen parkland is one of the most endangered habitats in Canada. The park is home to more than 40 species of mammals, including free-roaming plains bison, wood bison, moose, and elk. It is also home to at least 250 bird species, including red-eyed vireos, least

UKRAINIAN CULTURAL HERITAGE VILLAGE

WASKAHEGAN TRAIL

The 235-kilometre Waskahegan Trail loops between Fort Saskatchewan, Edmonton, and Camrose, using both public and private land. From Edmonton, the trail leads south along the Whitemud and Blackmud creeks, past Saunders and Coal lakes, to arrive in the Wetaskiwin area. The trail continues east along the Battle River from Gwynne to Camrose, and then north from Miquelon Lake through the Ministik Lake Bird Sanctuary, the Hastings Lake area, and the Cooking Lake–Blackfoot Provincial Recreation Area to Elk Island National Park before directing hikers west along Ross Creek to Fort Saskatchewan.

Sunday hikes are held on different trails throughout the year. Each hike usually covers about 10 kilometres and takes six to seven hours. Walking schedules are published on the Waskahegan Trail Association website (www.waskahegantrail.ca).

NOTE: Both domestic and wild animals may be encountered on the trail. Most of the trail is infrequently travelled, and in remote areas you will be far from immediate aid. There are no markers flagging potential hazards. Do not open any gates or travel off marked routes. Only walking-based activities such as hiking, skiing, and snowshoeing are permitted.

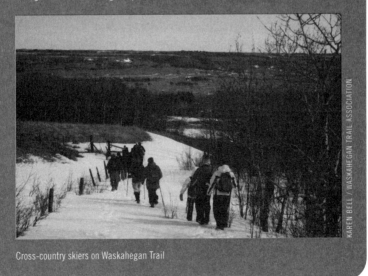

KAREN BELL / WASKAHEGAN TRAIL ASSOCIATION

Cross-country skiers on Waskahegan Trail

flycatchers, song sparrows, northern saw-whet and great horned owls, double-crested cormorants, great blue herons, and black-crowned night-herons. The red-necked grebe is the most common waterfowl species here, and the park is one of the few places outside the Rocky Mountains where Barrow's goldeneyes nest.

The park has an extensive cultural history: it contains the remains of homesteader cabins, the site of Alberta's first forest ranger station, and 227 Aboriginal sites—most of which are camp and stone-tool-making sites. Historic buildings in the park include the superintendent's home, a pavilion overlooking the beach, a horse barn, and a Ukrainian pioneer home.

In 1881–82, German, British, and Ukrainian settlers cleared land around the Beaver Hills, though not in them because they were too hilly and wet. The hills were important habitat for fur-trade animals until the 1830s, when beaver were virtually eliminated here. As late as 1841, bison were still taken in large numbers but were becoming scarce. Bison were almost eliminated by the late 1860s, and other large herbivores, such as moose and elk, became hard to find. Fire devastated the area in 1895, prompting the federal government to create the Cooking Lake Forest Reserve in 1899. Still, sport and sustenance hunting threatened wildlife populations, and the Beaver Hills elk became one of Canada's last intact herds. In 1906, the federal government established Elk Park and erected a 2.2-metre-high fence to create the first federally controlled big game sanctuary in Canada. It became a national park in 1930, and is Canada's only national park that is completely surrounded by a fence.

Every year, park staff round up the bison population, re-creating a practice that dates back almost 100 years. The herds are vaccinated and checked for disease, and surplus animals are culled for sale at auction. For many years, herd reductions took the form of slaughter, and the meat went to Aboriginal bands across Canada and overseas armed forces during World War II. On occasion it was sold through retail outlets. These practices ended in the mid-1960s, when shooting animals in national parks became less acceptable to the public.

The information centre near the south gate is open daily during the summer. You can see park history and natural heritage displays, pick up a trail map, and learn about interpretive program and special event schedules. There are 11 self-guided trails that thread through more than 100 kilometres of lakes, spruce bogs, low-forested hills, and meadows. Trails vary from short strolls on a boardwalk to the scenic 18.6-kilometre Wood Bison Trail. The paved Shoreline Trail is wheelchair accessible. The park is available to day visitors, and a weekly junior naturalist program is held for children aged 7 to 12 during the summer. Hiking trails are used for cross-country skiing in the winter.

COOKING LAKE–BLACKFOOT PROVINCIAL RECREATION AREA

Distance: 46 km, or about 40 minutes, east of Edmonton on Hwy 16, immediately south of and adjacent to Elk Island National Park.

Info: The park recreation area is open daily from 7 a.m. to 11 p.m. The interpretive centre is located at the Waskahegan Staging Area on Range Road 210, 7 km south of Hwy 16. It is typically open daily in the summer season, during special events, or at other times when volunteers become available. Phone 780-922-1153, or call the Trails Update information line at 780-922-4676. Bring your own firewood. Potable water is not available in the backcountry. Visit www.dotheblackfoot.ca/events.htm, or call to ask about special events and tours to orient you to the area.

The Cooking Lake–Blackfoot Provincial Recreation Area was once a major hunting ground for Sarcee, Cree, and Blackfoot tribes. Today this 97-square-kilometre region is enjoyed for its more than 170 kilometres of backcountry trails through forest, pasture, and wetland areas. A multi-use area, it supports agriculture, wildlife management, and natural gas extraction, as well as outdoor recreation, including horseback riding, cross-country skiing, hiking, mountain biking, and dogsledding. Canada's largest cross-country ski event, the Canadian Birkebeiner Ski Festival, is held here every February.

The park's four day-use areas—Blackfoot, Central, Islet Lake, and Waskehegan—have all-weather shelters, warm-up stoves, washrooms, firepits, and picnic facilities. Cold, running water is available in summer. There are 19 trails and numerous birdwatching sites, with more than 200 species of birds, including two pairs of trumpeter swans that have been known to nest here. The world's largest and rarest swan, trumpeters are a vulnerable species in Alberta. Watch for bluebirds, red-tailed hawks, northern flickers, and great blue herons, and be careful not to disturb the nesting sites of any birds. You can pick up a bird checklist and trail guide at the Cooking Lake–Blackfoot Heritage Interpretive Centre while checking out the exhibits depicting forest ranger activities, farm implements, and area history. Trail maps are also available at kiosks located at each staging area.

The Cooking Lake Forest Reserve, founded in 1899, includes the landmass we know today as Cooking Lake–Blackfoot Recreation Area and Elk Island National Park.

Visitors can enjoy canoeing and kayaking on Islet Lake, as well as horseback riding on 85 kilometres of equestrian trails and in designated pastures. Blackfoot Staging Area equestrian trails can be used for mushing (dogsledding) and skijoring (skiing while being towed by a horse) in winter. The 5 Peaks Trail Running company has added Blackfoot to its series of running events. Another major event is the Ultra Marathon held every May, with marathoners nicknaming the Siksika Trail "death by a thousand hills."

Blackfoot Staging Area and Beaver Hills Dark Sky Preserve

Location: 4 km east of the Elk Island National Park entrance and about 0.8 km east of the Ukrainian Heritage Village entrance. Turn south at the first crossroads onto Range Road 195 and travel 4 km to the park entrance. The observing area is 0.5 km past the cattle guard. Drive slowly to avoid running into anyone—or their telescopes—as well as to keep dust to a minimum.

Info: Observing sessions are usually held the weekend prior to a new moon. There is no fee. It is imperative to follow night sky etiquette to avoid diminishing participants' night vision. For more information, visit the Royal Astronomical Society website at www.edmontonrasc.com/edsblackfoot.html.

The Blackfoot Provincial Recreation Area is a 300-square-kilometre region east of Sherwood Park dedicated to maintaining dark skies. The preserve encompasses Elk Island National Park and the Cooking Lake–Blackfoot Provincial Recreation Area. The Royal

NIGHT SKY ETIQUETTE

It takes up to 30 minutes to regain night vision after exposure to white light. When approaching a dark site for stargazing, it is considered good etiquette to take the following measures:

- Turn off, disable, or cover up exterior vehicle headlights and pause for about 5 to 10 minutes to let your eyes adjust to the darkness. If you cannot disable all interior lights, honk or shout "white light!" a few seconds before opening vehicle doors at the site.
- Use a red flashlight when light is needed.
- Park at the gate for a minimum of 5 to 10 minutes because it takes 30 to 60 minutes to adapt fully to darkness. Roll down your window and use a red flashlight to illuminate the road.
- Stop completely before entering the staging area. Walk around to locate people and equipment before choosing a parking spot. Because backup lights are white, try to park so that you can leave without backing up or using your brakes.
- Do not smoke on the observing field because it damages telescope optics, and flames from matches and lighters affect dark-adapted eyes.
- Do not use insect repellent spray or other aerosol sprays on the observing field. A single drop of spray can permanently damage telescope optics.
- When leaving an observation site, do not turn on car headlights until after exiting the parking area. If lights cannot be deactivated, cover them with a cloth or paper bag.
- Do not use flash photography, which can destroy night vision for 45 minutes to an hour.

Astronomical Society of Canada hosts observing sessions that are open to the public.

FORT SASKATCHEWAN

Directions: Exit Edmonton on Hwy 16 east, and turn onto Hwy 21 north.
Distance: 38.7 km, or about 35 minutes, from Edmonton.
Info: www.fortsask.ca

More than 200 years ago, the Fort Saskatchewan area was known for canoe building, thanks to the raw materials found near the mouth of the Sturgeon River in the Birch Hills. Anthony Henday camped here in spring 1755 to prepare for his trip back to the Hudson Bay.

In 1795, the North West Company built Fort Augustus across the river from present-day Fort Saskatchewan. The rival Hudson's Bay Company established its Edmonton House uncomfortably near, but by 1802 the fur trade was no longer profitable, and both forts relocated. A 1926 stone cairn overlooks the river flats, marking the site where the trading posts once stood.

After an exhausting trek across the prairies, the North West Mounted Police (NWMP) arrived in the area in 1874. In 1875, Inspector W. O. Jarvis built Sturgeon Creek Post, which later became Fort Saskatchewan—named from the Cree word for swift current. It was the area's first North West Mounted Police post and the second post in what was still the Northwest Territories. Though Edmonton residents wanted the post built closer to them, this site was chosen because the Canadian Pacific Railway was expected to cross the river nearby. The railway's plan eventually changed but the post remained, and the Seventh Company of the 65th Montreal Rifles protected the fort during the 1885 Riel Rebellion. Afterwards, the North West Mounted Police presence was increased, and by year-end the fort became G Division headquarters. When the division was transferred to Edmonton in 1913, the Alberta government bought the site and built a gaol that opened in 1915. It held prisoners sentenced to less than two years and a day, as well as those remanded and awaiting trial; 29 prisoners were executed here between 1916 and 1960.

Fort Saskatchewan became a town in 1904 and was linked to Edmonton by a demanding dirt trail that wound around sloughs and woodlands. One fall morning in 1905, 170 wagon teams made their way along this well-used route. The Canadian Northern Railway arrived in 1905, and the town flourished as it became an established point on the transcontinental line from the east. By 1911 the town had 49 businesses and an $8,000 opera house. Transportation improved further when the road to Edmonton was gravelled in 1926, oiled in 1930, and paved in 1950. This was a time when mixed-gender drinking was allowed in Fort Saskatchewan but not in Edmonton, so you can imagine the popularity of this thoroughfare.

Sherritt Gordon Mines built a multi-million-dollar nickel refinery in Fort Saskatchewan in 1952. Growth of the town continued at a steady pace when petrochemical industries moved into the area, drawn to land availability, transportation access, salt deposits, and water supply. Fort Saskatchewan became a city in 1985. Today, the city and surrounding area are home to more than 21 light and heavy industrial plants.

Despite its city status, Fort Saskatchewan has taken a decidedly rural approach to cutting grass and controlling weeds. Guided by a shepherd, the city keeps a flock of 50 sheep to graze city lands. You can visit the friendly flock of living lawnmowers from Thursday to Sunday, 12 p.m. to 8 p.m., from early June to the Labour Day holiday in early September. The flock grazes the areas next to Legacy Park (99th Avenue and 101st Street), behind the Fort Saskatchewan Museum and Historic Site (100th Avenue and 100th Street), beside the Warden's House (Visitor Information Centre, at 100th Avenue and 100 Street), along the River Valley Amphitheatre and toward the river, as well as the Nordic Ski Centre (Agrium's greenbelt) on River Road, from where the flock is herded to Legacy Park on Thursdays at noon. (780-992-6261.)

DIANE YANCH

Young visitors play with the sheep at Fort Saskatchewan

The picnic tables outside the Fort Saskatchewan railway station and grounds (10030–99th Avenue) are a nice place to stop for a rest. The original Canadian National Railway (CNR) stationmaster's office and upstairs living quarters are nicely restored, and a 1957 caboose sits on an original piece of track outside the station, which now houses the Fort Saskatchewan Chamber of Commerce. You can see the station during the chamber's operating hours, which are 8 a.m. to 5 p.m. from Monday to Friday. (780-998-4355.)

Annual Fort Saskatchewan events include Canada Day Celebrations, with an antique car show, antique snowmobile show, Legacy Park Family Festival, Neighbour Day, and Santa Claus Parade.

Fort Saskatchewan Museum and Historic Site

Location: 10006–100th Avenue, Fort Saskatchewan.
Info: Open daily 10 a.m. to 4 p.m. Guided tours year-round. Admission charged. 780-998-1783.

Here you'll find the Fort Saskatchewan Visitor Information Centre, as well as the museum and historic site, which includes eight heritage buildings in a 1.2-hectare (3-acre) village overlooking the North Saskatchewan River. Located near Legacy Park, Jarvis Park, and the historic CNR station, the buildings are furnished with period furniture and radiate the feeling of a bygone era. You can picnic here or visit one of several nearby downtown restaurants.

The museum's central building is a brick courthouse, which was built for $20,000 in 1909. The artifacts here depict local North West Mounted Police history. You will also find an authentic farmhouse of the era, doctor's residence, church, school, and machinery shed.

Stratotech Park International Raceway

Location: 55112 Secondary Hwy 825, Sturgeon Industrial Park, Fort Saskatchewan.
Info: Raceway hours: April to October, Monday through Sunday, noon to dusk. 780-485-9751 (Edmonton office) or 780-998-9995 (raceway); www.stratotech.ca.

Stratotech Park International Raceway is a complete kart, formula, and sport bike racing facility. It was awarded the MAX AWARD for Best Track at the North American International Motor Cycle Super Show in 2003 and hosted northern Alberta's first Canadian National Karting Championship in 2006.

GIBBONS

Directions: Exit Edmonton on Hwy 28A, north.
Distance: 39.7 km, or about 38 minutes, from Edmonton.
Info: www.gibbons.ca.

Gibbons Museum

Location: 4709–48th Avenue, Gibbons.
Info: Open July through September, Wednesday to Sunday, 9:30 a.m. to 5:30 p.m. Will provide tours Mondays and Tuesdays if pre-arranged. Wheelchair accessible

Gibbons Museum run by the Sturgeon River Historical Society

for pre-arranged tours. You can also explore independently. 780-923-2148 or 780-923-3503.

Visit the Gibbons Museum for a look at historic buildings dating from the town's settlement, including an original log home, a settler's home, a barn, and the McLean Brothers Store, as well as equipment, tools, and artifacts. Tables available for picnicking.

Great Prairie Corn Maze—Prairie Gardens & Greenhouses

Location: 56311 Lily Lake Road, Bon Accord. Travel north on Hwy 28A and west on Hwy 28 about 4 km.
Info: Admission charged. 780-921-2272.

Five kilometres of twisting, turning trails wind through 2.5 hectares (6 acres) of corn at the Great Prairie Corn Maze. A number of activities are included with admission, including a short maze adventure lasting about 15 minutes, Straw Mountain, a petting farm, play areas, a straw-bale maze, tractor driven wagon rides, gem mining, and a haunted house. You can explore 10 hectares (25 acres) of gardens,

U-pick areas, and a gift shop. Make sure to call ahead to find out the best time to visit. Remember to wear sturdy shoes when planning to trek through a corn maze.

SMOKY LAKE

Directions: Exit Edmonton on Hwy 28A north and continue straight onto Hwy 28 east.
Distance: 116 km, or about 1 hour and 33 minutes, from Edmonton.
Info: 780-656-3674; www.smokylake.ca.

A town of just over 1,000 people, Smoky Lake calls itself the Pumpkin Capital of Alberta, and the Western Gateway to the Iron Horse Trail—a 300-kilometre stretch that runs through northeast Alberta. Open year-round, the trail supports hiking, mountain biking, cross-country skiing, and horseback riding, as well as all-terrain vehicle and snowmobile use. It is part of the Trans Canada Trail and Trans Canadian Snowmobile Trail systems.

Archaeological finds indicate that Cree people lived here at least 6,000 years ago. Although the area was busy with trapping and trading in the early 1800s, the settlement that became Smoky Lake did not originate until 1862 when the Methodist Church established a mission along the North Saskatchewan River. The Hudson's Bay Company followed with a fur-trading post and by 1915 the area was heavily settled. The Victoria Trail, which follows the North Saskatchewan River, was used to transport goods by wagon from Fort Saskatchewan and Fort Edmonton, and some local farmers living along the route opened stores in their homes.

When the anticipated railway bypassed the settlement and came north through what is now the town of Smoky Lake, settlers relocated to be near the railway. Smoky Lake became a hamlet in 1917, an incorporated village in 1923, and a town in 1962. Today the historic Smoky Lake Canadian National Railway Station houses tourist information and an art gallery.

The town takes its name from the 19-kilometre-long lake located approximately 5 kilometres west of town. Some believe the Cree called the lake Smoking Lake because it is often covered in a haze that looks like rising smoke; others say the Cree named it Smoking Place because they gathered near the lake to smoke pipes when hunting.

Smoky Lake was once known for having the most businesses per capita anywhere in Canada and is so identified in *Ripley's Believe It or Not*. With a population of just 250 between 1930 and 1940, the town thrived with various businesses that included a butcher shop, a brick factory, a flour mill, a photo studio, and implement dealers.

Smoky Lake hosts Stampede and Heritage Days in August but is best known for its annual Great White North Pumpkin Fair on the first Saturday in October. One of the largest pumpkin festivals in North America, competitors from across Alberta, British Columbia, and Saskatchewan haul their largest gourds here for the chance to win a prize for growing the heaviest pumpkin, squash, or watermelon. Prize-winning pumpkins of more than 1,000 pounds have challenged Smoky Lake scales. Be sure to take some photos in Pumpkin Park, where you will find seven giant, bright orange cement gourds. (The Pumpkin Hotline: 780-656-3674; Alberta Lakeland: 1-888-645-4155; town@ town.smokylake.ab.ca.)

Smoky Lake CN Museum and Tourist Information

Location: West Railway Drive and Wheatland Avenue by Flag Park, Smoky Lake.
Info: Open daily from May through the Labour Day weekend, 10 a.m. to 6 p.m. Donations appreciated. 780-656-3674.

The Smoky Lake CN Museum and tourist information is set in the town's 1919 CNR station, complete with a wooden platform, potbellied stove, and ticket-agent wicket, where return trips to Edmonton were once sold for $1.95. You can see a telegraph logbook and baggage room, complete with a collection of baggage on a trolley ready to be loaded onto a train. As well as collecting visitor information, you can view the White Earth Art Gallery, featuring the work of local artists. Open July and August. (780-656-3918.)

Smoky Lake Museum

Location: From Hwy 28, take the second right entrance into Smoky Lake and turn left after about 100 metres.
Info: Open Victoria Day to Labour Day, Saturdays and Sundays, from 1 p.m. to 5 p.m. Partial wheelchair access. Admission by donation. Phone 780-656-3510 to make access arrangements during weekdays and in the off-season. Tours offered by appointment.

Housed in the old Victoria School, the Smoky Lake Museum contains numerous artifacts from the community's pioneer days, including some of the many items Ukrainian immigrants and other early settlers brought to the area. The museum also showcases a selection of a local artist's private taxidermy collection of animals, including birds, plus early settler machinery and the restored Pakan Ferry.

Victoria Trail

Location: East of Fort Saskatchewan on Hwy 15; turn left (north) on Hwy 830. Turn left (west) on Hwy 38, cross the Vinca Bridge, and continue west until you see the sign for Victoria Trail. Turn right onto Victoria Trail and follow the directional and interpretive signs along its length.
Info: Pick up a guide of Kalyna Country's Historical Walking & Driving Tour of Victoria Trail at visitor information centres and select outlets in Kalyna Country.

The 58-kilometre historic Victoria Trail is the oldest road in Alberta still in use. Aboriginal people first used the trail along the North Saskatchewan River banks. Explorers, fur traders, and Ukrainian settlers followed, travelling by foot, horse, cart, or buggy to reach their new homesteads.

No longer a primitive route, the Victoria Trail winds through scenic farmland from Secondary Highway 38, southeast of Redwater, to the Victoria Settlement Provincial Historic Site in Smoky Lake County. It

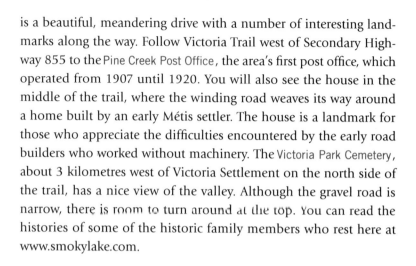

is a beautiful, meandering drive with a number of interesting landmarks along the way. Follow Victoria Trail west of Secondary Highway 855 to the Pine Creek Post Office, the area's first post office, which operated from 1907 until 1920. You will also see the house in the middle of the trail, where the winding road weaves its way around a home built by an early Métis settler. The house is a landmark for those who appreciate the difficulties encountered by the early road builders who worked without machinery. The Victoria Park Cemetery, about 3 kilometres west of Victoria Settlement on the north side of the trail, has a nice view of the valley. Although the gravel road is narrow, there is room to turn around at the top. You can read the histories of some of the historic family members who rest here at www.smokylake.com.

Victoria Settlement Provincial Historic Site

Location: 10 km south of Smoky Lake on Secondary Hwy 855, and then 6 km east on the historic Victoria Trail.

Info: From May 15 to the Labour Day weekend, open daily from 10 a.m. to 6 p.m. Admission charged. Tours are always available. Fur-trade games and other special activities can be arranged by calling ahead. 780-656-2333 (mid-May to Labour Day); 780-645-6256 (winter).

Victoria Settlement was one of the first three provincial historic sites to be named in Alberta and is home to the province's oldest building that is still in its original location—the fully restored and furnished 1864 Hudson's Bay Company clerk quarters. The Hudson's Bay Company established Fort Victoria to trade axes and other staples with Aboriginals who brought pelts, hides, and bison meat. The settlement is also the site where Reverend George McDougall founded a Methodist Mission in 1862 to serve the Cree. The mission and fort became the centre of activity for Métis who lived on river lots along the North Saskatchewan River.

The interpretive centre is located in the 1906 Methodist Church and Hudson's Bay clerk quarters. Costumed interpreters explain area history, such as the terrible smallpox epidemic of 1870, in which 55 members of the community perished. On Thursdays and Saturdays historical demonstrations may include wood-stove–baking, wood bending, or other early skills and crafts. Special events are offered on various weekends during the summer.

Métis Crossing

Location: 13 km south of Smoky Lake, at the intersection of Hwy 855 and Victoria Trail. Exit Smoky Lake on Hwy 855 south and drive to the Victoria Trail intersection. **Info:** Open Victoria Day to Labour Day, 11 a.m. to 6 p.m. Admission charged. 780-656-2229.

Métis Crossing is an Aboriginal interpretive centre on a 207-hectare (512 acre) site on the banks of the North Saskatchewan River, 4 kilometres west of Victoria Settlement. You will find a re-created fort and tipi village with costumed Métis interpreters who explain life as it was lived in the late 1800s and demonstrate mid-1900s farming methods. Expect to enjoy a warm Métis welcome with some fiddling and jigging at this National Historic Site. You can learn how to make bannock and scrape a hide, or ride a Red River cart or York boat. There is a roughly 1-kilometre-long nature trail to explore, and a beautiful riverfront spot with picnic tables.

ANDREW

Directions: Exit Edmonton on Hwy 16 east, turn left at Hwy 15, continue on Hwy 855 (through Sawchuk Street in Mundare), and continue on Range Road 164. **Distance:** 116 km, or about 1 hour and 23 minutes, from Edmonton. **Info:** 780-365-3687

Andrew is home to the premier of Alberta, the Honourable Ed Stelmach. It is also home to the world's largest mallard duck—a 1-ton creation with a wingspan of 7.2 metres (23 feet)—located in the Lions Club Park on the southeast corner of Highways 855 and 45. The giant duck was built in 1992 in honour of area wetlands such as nearby Whitford Lake, 3 kilometres northwest of Andrew. The lake is a popular breeding ground for mallards and is part of a migration flyway; it serves as a rest and refuelling stop for birds flying hundreds and sometimes thousands of kilometres on routes that span North America.

Whitford Lake has three watchable wildlife sites with viewing platforms, signed trails, and boardwalks. Birders will especially enjoy visiting here during spring and fall migration. Look high up to spot flocks of mallards—at 6,400 metres, they have one of the highest migration heights.

Andrew is home to a very well-preserved grain elevator, which houses the Andrew Grain Elevator Interpretive Centre. A provincial historic site, the elevator contains displays and artifacts related to the early grain trade and the area's rural life. An annual family corn roast is held in August. Open from June through September, Saturday and Sunday, noon to 4 p.m., or by appointment year-round. Admission charged. Phone 780-365-3236 or 780-365-2237 for tours.

The intriguing Andrew Museum (5043–52nd Street) is located in the old Canadian Pacific Railway Station. Visitors will see artifacts, farm machinery, hand tools, and late-19th-century European clothing from countries including Germany, Romania, Poland, and different areas of Ukraine. Admission charged. Phone 780-365-2237 to have the doors opened and arrange a tour.

WILLINGDON AREA

Historical Village and Pioneer Museum at Shandro

Directions: Exit Edmonton on Hwy 16 east, turn left at Hwy 15, and continue on Hwy 855/Sawchuk Street; turn right at Hwy 29 (637), turn left at Hwy 857, and turn left again at Hwy 45/Hwy 857.

Distance: About 9 km from Willingdon and 134 km from Edmonton.

Info: Open in the summer, from the Canada Day weekend to the Labour Day

weekend, Friday to Monday, 10 a.m. to 6 p.m. 780-367-2283 or call Wilson at
780-367-2428 to make arrangements in spring and fall. Village of Willingdon:
780-367-2337.

Most Willingdon-area settlers were of Ukrainian and Romanian origin. Their history comes to life at the Historical Village and Pioneer
Museum at Shandro. This 19-building site includes a fully furnished
Orthodox church, which pioneers began building in 1899. There is
a sod hut (circa 1899) and a log home with a thatched roof (circa
1902), as well as a working blacksmith shop. The buildings are furnished with early-1900s artifacts, utensils, handicrafts, clothing,
accessories, furniture, equipment, and tools. Most of these were
brought to Canada from the Ukraine in the late 18th and early 19th
centuries, or made by immigrants who settled here.

BRUDERHEIM

Directions: Exit Edmonton on Hwy 16 east, turn onto Hwy 21 north, and continue
through Fort Saskatchewan on what becomes Hwy 15 east; turn left at Hwy 45/
Range Road 204 and follow Hwy 45 to Bruderheim.
Distance: 61.9 km, or about 52 minutes, from Edmonton.
Info: 780-796-3731; www.bruderheim.ca.

Bruderheim was founded in 1894 by German-speaking immigrants
from Volhynia, Russia. Situated between the North Saskatchewan
River and Highway 15, the community has grown in recent years,
more than tripling since 1974 due to the growth of nearby petrochemical plants. Today just over 1,200 people live in this farming
community on Lamont County's west boundary—an area known
worldwide for its prize livestock and grain.

Bruderheim is also recognized for its Moravian Church, which
is home to a branch of one of the oldest Protestant denominations,
dating back to 1457. In 1895, Andreas Lilge, a teacher and lay leader
in Volhynia, wanted to bring Volhynian Moravians to Canada, where

religious freedom was guaranteed and Christians could establish communities. Approximately 100 families decided to move, and the first immigrants arrived in 1883. They erected a log church in 1886, which is still standing although no longer used. It is being converted into the Canadian Moravian Museum. (A newer church on the site is typically open from 9 a.m. to noon, Monday through Friday, as well as on Sunday mornings for services.) Services were once held in German, Norwegian, Russian, and Ukrainian as well as English. You will find an Alberta government information sign on Highway 15 and some printed information about the Moravians inside both churches. (5124–48th Street; 780-796-3775; usually open Tuesdays.)

LAMONT

Directions: Exit Edmonton on Hwy 16 east, turn onto Hwy 21 north toward Fort Saskatchewan, and continue on 89th Avenue/Hwy 15 east.
Distance: 67.3 km, or about 57 minutes, from Edmonton.
Info: www.lamont.ca.

Incorporated as a town in 1968, Lamont was named in 1906 in honour of Justice J. H. Lamont, a native of Ontario who became a lawyer and moved to Prince Albert in 1899. He became its Member of Parliament for a year and later ran for the Legislative Assembly when Saskatchewan became a province. From 1905 to 1907, Lamont served as Saskatchewan's first Attorney General and was later appointed Judge of the Supreme Court of Saskatchewan. He was appointed to the Supreme Court of Canada in 1927.

Lamont County is part of the Kalyna Country Ecomuseum, a living outdoor museum that encompasses some 20,000 kilometres.

Home to Canada's oldest and largest agricultural settlement of Ukrainians, and encompassing 27 townships, Lamont County has more churches per capita than any other region in North America. The county is home to 47 churches that mark the intensely spiritual heritage of the eastern European settlers who journeyed here in the late 1800s and early 1900s. The Lamont County Church Tour takes visitors through villages and towns, and along country roads where early pioneers made sacrifices to build churches and express their deep faith, including Eastern Rites and a number of Christian denominations. You can expect to see a variety of architectural styles, interior detail, and art, as well as freestanding bell towers and the unique onion-shaped domes that Ukrainian settlers built in the Byzantine tradition. Tour booklets are available at the Lamont County Office, all town and village offices in the county, visitor centres, and museums, and at various main street locations in participating towns. You can also visit www.lamontcounty.ca or www.kalynacountry.com (or call 1-877-895-2233 or 1-888-452-5962) for a church tour booklet, maps, and an itinerary for the annual Doors Open event, during which participating churches welcome visitors to tour the churches' interiors.

MUNDARE

Directions: Exit Edmonton on Hwy 16 east, and turn left at Hwy 15.
Distance: 84.1 km, or about 57 minutes, from Edmonton.
Info: www.mundare.ca.

An especially fertile farming region, Mundare was settled primarily by former pioneers originating from Halychyna, an area in Ukraine with similar soil and climatic conditions. Murals throughout the town depict Mundare's Ukrainian cultural and agricultural history, while the Basilian Fathers Museum preserves Ukrainian customs and religious heritage.

For a rest stop, consider Ukraina Park, which has a covered area with picnic tables. You will also find picnic tables at the tourist information rest area (Sawchuk Street and 50th Avenue) under the Giant Kubassa known as the World's Largest Ukrainian Sausage. This 12.8-metre (42 foot) statue honours Stawnichy's Meat Processing, a family sausage business that started in 1959 in a small grocery store. Today the company smokes sausages in a meat-processing plant that goes through about 9,072 kilograms (20,000 pounds) of pork each week, and about 27,215 kilograms (60,000 pounds) each week in the lead- up to Christmas. You can visit Stawnichy's at 5212–50th Street.

On the south side of Highway 16, 4 kilometres east of Mundare, the Parkland Conservation Farm welcomes visitors to explore its natural area and walk the Agriculture Adventure Trail and Aspen Parkland Trail. (780-632-2244; www.parklandconservationfarm.com.)

Basilian Fathers Museum

Location: 5335 Sawchuk Street, Mundare.
Info: Open year-round on weekdays, 10 a.m. to 4 p.m. Open on the weekends in the summer, 1 p.m. to 5 p.m. Cameras are not allowed in galleries. Donations welcomed. 780-764-3887; www.basilianmuseum.org.

The Ukrainian Catholic Church in Canada established its first missionary centre in Mundare. When the Communist regime severed contact with Ukraine in the 1940s, the Basilians wanted to preserve the cultural and religious heritage of Ukrainians in Canada. They achieved this by opening the Basilian Fathers Museum in 1957. The Fathers demonstrated their ongoing commitment by building a new facility in 1991 to mark the centenary of Ukrainian settlement in Canada.

The museum shares the intriguing history of the Basilian order, which takes its name from St. Basil—the fourth-century bishop who launched the first monastic rules in what is now Turkey. Exhibits take visitors back to the 10th century, when Ukrainians adopted Christianity, and portray the history of the Basilian Fathers' mission in east-central Alberta. The museum traces the Ukrainian Catholic Church's development in Canada from 1902 to the present. It includes Ukrainian settlement history, and presents folk relics and Ukrainian Catholic religious artifacts including chalices, vestments, candle holders, and a collection of 16th- and 17th-century liturgical books from

Ukraine. Some date from as far back as the 15th century. Be sure to note the original 18th- and 19th-century icons painted on wood panels. The museum also has a library, archives, and gift shop.

Walk across the road from the museum to view the outside of the Basilian Fathers Monastery—Canada's oldest Basilian Monastery—built in 1922. The 1933 grotto, shrine, and garden are still used to celebrate Divine Liturgies. In its busiest period, the monastery was home to more than 50 members. On the last Sunday in June, the Feast of Saints Peter and Paul is celebrated with a liturgy at the grotto.

VEGREVILLE

Directions: Exit Edmonton on Hwy 16 east, and access the town via the Hwy 16A east exit toward Vegreville.
Distance: 102 km, or about 1 hour and 9 minutes, from Edmonton.
Info: www.vegreville.com.

The community of Vegreville was named in honour of Father Valentin Vegreville of the Oblates of Mary Immaculate (OMI), a missionary who began serving western Canada in the early 1850s.

Vegreville's first settlers arrived in April 1894. French-Canadians came from Kansas and were joined by English families from the United States and Eastern Canada. Emigrants followed from Eastern and Central Europe, as well as the British Isles.

Vegreville's post office opened in December 1895, and the Canadian Northern Railway came within 7.25 kilometres northeast of the hamlet by 1905. Anxious to take advantage of rail transportation, the residents moved their buildings to be near the tracks. Incorporated as a town in 1906, Vegreville eventually became a centre for Ukrainian settlement. More than 30 different ethnic groups lived here by the 1950s, the largest of which were British, French, German, and Ukrainian. For many dozens of years, Vegreville's northeast area was known as French Town.

Today, just over 5,300 people live in Vegreville. The town marks the southern point of Alberta's largest Ukrainian bloc settlement—the Kalyna Country Ecomuseum. You can explore Vegreville's history on its restored main street, where plaques embedded in the sidewalk note a major community event for each year from 1905 to 2004. Also downtown, the Rotary Peace Park contains Peace Grove, 12 trees dedicated to promoting world peace through tourism. The town's visitor information centre is located in Elks/Kinsmen Park, adjacent to the Vegreville municipal campground, where you will find picnic spots and site stoves, as well as a cook shack, gazebo, and skate park. It's easy to find. Just look for the statue of a giant Easter egg!

The world's largest *pysanka* (a Ukrainian Easter egg) is the most intricate and beautiful of all the large monuments in Alberta. Set on a 12,150-kilogram (27,000 pound) pedestal that allows the egg to turn in the wind like a weathervane, the pysanka is 7.71 metres (25.7 feet) long, 5.4 metres (18 feet) wide, and 9.3 metres (31 feet) high. It has a 900-kilogram (2,000 pound) aluminum skin attached to a central mast at a 30-degree angle, with 177 turnbuckle struts and a colossal 1,350-kilogram (3,000 pound) internal structure. Decorated in traditional Ukrainian style, the egg's exquisite colours and intricate symbols stand for harmony, vitality, and culture. It contains 524 star patterns, 1,108 equilateral triangles, 3,512 visible facets, 6,978 nuts and bolts, and 177 internal struts.

Built in 1975 to commemorate the Royal Canadian Mounted Police Centennial, the egg symbolizes the peace and security that Mounties provided to the region's pioneers and descendants. You will find the giant *pysanka* in the Elks/Kinsmen Park, north on 43rd Street, just off Highway 16A, on Vegreville's east end. The tourist information centre is also located in the park.

When travelling on Highway 16A east of Vegreville, about 0.8 kilometres east of the pysanka, watch for the Our Lady of the Highway Shrine. Built by the Knights of Columbus, the shrine is dedicated to the Blessed Virgin Mary to offer travellers protection. The figure is sculpted from Italian white marble, and beautifully marked stones display the Stations of the Cross around the statue.

Vegreville Regional Museum and International Police Museum

Location: 1 km east of Vegreville on Hwy 16A.
Info: Hours subject to change. Phone ahead. 780-632-7650. Admission by donation.

The Vegreville Regional Museum explores area history beginning in 1890, and examines how the region's agricultural base and mix of British, French, German, and Ukrainian pioneers contributed to this prairie community. The Right Honourable Donald F. Mazankowski, P.C. Collection exhibits 25 years of the distinguished public service of this former deputy prime minister of Canada. The Vegreville and District Sports Hall of Fame and the International Police Museum are also housed here. If time permits, consider a stroll through the museum grounds or the nearby bird sanctuary, which is situated along the Vermillion River.

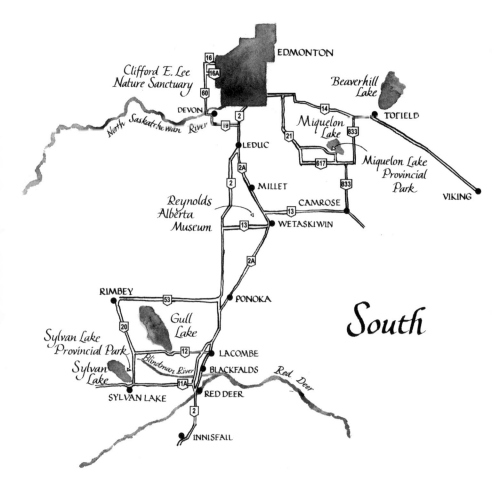

EDMONTON

16
16A

Clifford E. Lee
Nature Sanctuary

60

DEVON

North Saskatchewan River

19

2

LEDUC

2A

2

MILLET

Reynolds
Alberta
Museum

13

13

WETASKIWIN

Beaverhill
Lake

14

TOFIELD

Miquelon
Lake

833

21

617

Miquelon Lake
Provincial
Park

833

CAMROSE

13

VIKING

2A

RIMBEY

53

PONOKA

Gull
Lake

20

Sylvan Lake
Provincial Park

12

LACOMBE

Blindman River

BLACKFALDS

Red Deer

Sylvan
Lake

11A

SYLVAN LAKE

RED DEER

2

South

INNISFAIL

SOUTH OF EDMONTON

Predominantly parkland, the area south of Edmonton includes sites in and around Devon, Leduc, Wetaskiwin, Camrose, Viking, Tofield, Lacombe, Red Deer, and Innisfail. The Oilfield Loop includes the history-altering Leduc Oil Well No. 1 and the Canadian Petroleum Interpretive Centre. The town of Devon, established to accommodate the needs of the oil boom after the drilling of Imperial Oil's Discovery Well, offers numerous recreational opportunities in the North Saskatchewan River valley, including one of the world's top ten water-skiing facilities.

Millet, which promotes itself as Alberta's prettiest little town, has numerous gardens and historic buildings that make it well worth a visit on the way to Wetaskiwin. Well known for the Reynolds-Alberta Museum and Canada's Aviation Hall of Fame, Wetaskiwin is also home to an intriguing legend that explains the origin of the town's name (read more about it on page 108).

Camrose, known as the Rose City, lies in the gently rolling agricultural parkland east of Wetaskiwin. A city of history and beauty, Camrose has numerous historic buildings and Alberta's Littlest Airport—a unique model-airplane and race-car facility.

Birding opportunities abound throughout the region. Miquelon Lake Provincial Park has been a designated bird sanctuary since the 1920s, and Beaverhill Lake provides feeding and resting habitat for more than 50,000 birds each year. A natural protected area, Beaverhill Lake offers a good example of a parkland pothole lake ecosystem in its natural state. Farther east again (this time toward a town named for its pirating ancestors), Viking boasts both hockey fame and

SIMPLE SUMMER FAMILY DAY TRIP
Total driving time: about 3 hours and 40 minutes

Make the **Reynolds-Alberta Museum and Canada's Aviation Hall of Fame** (page 112) in Wetaskiwin your first stop on a jaunt south of Edmonton. Enjoy lunch at Huckleberry's Café (3840 56 Street), then head toward Camrose, stopping to stretch and see the swans and Viking longship at **Mirror Lake Park** (page 93). If you're in the area on a weekend, there's a good chance of seeing model aircraft operators as they fly planes and race cars at **Alberta's Littlest Airport** (page 95). The action will be even better if you time your visit with one of their major events. Now drive to **Miquelon Lake Provincial Park** (page 95), and plan to explore nature and enjoy a picnic supper before heading back to Edmonton.

historic petroglyphs, carved into a grouping of quartzite boulders at least 1,000 years ago.

To the south, Lacombe has numerous sites and attractions, including Alberta's most intact Edwardian main street. You can also visit Michener House Museum, where former Governor General of Canada Roland Michener was born. From here, the highway leads to Red Deer, Alberta's third-largest city and a place where planning a day trip will mean picking and choosing what to see with each visit. You might enjoy the Sports Hall of Fame, a ghost tour, numerous outdoor opportunities, or a visit to the Norwegian Laft Hus to discover distinctive Norwegian-Canadian culture. The next stop is Innisfail, where Anthony Henday first saw the Rocky Mountains. If you time it carefully, you might see a police dog training demonstration. Innisfail is also home to the only stopping house preserved from the days of stagecoach travel between Calgary and Edmonton.

Highway 2 between Edmonton and Calgary was named the Queen Elizabeth II Highway on May 23, 2005. Locally, this 260-kilometre section of highway is referred to as the Queen-E, QEW, or Q-E. It is the longest continuous roadway in Canada to be named after a monarch, and the only road to be named after Queen Elizabeth II, as Ontario's Queen Elizabeth Way is named after the Queen Mother. The Queen personally unveiled the first new road sign.

LEDUC

Directions: Exit Edmonton on Hwy 2 south, and choose Exit 519 to Leduc.
Distance: 35.4 km, or about 37 minutes, from Edmonton.
Info: 780-980-7127; www.leduc.ca.

Leduc's first settler, Robert Taylor Telford, came to this picturesque prairie parkland in 1889. The area's first postmaster, general merchant, and justice of the peace, Telford later served as mayor and Member of the Legislative Assembly. The settlement was informally called Telford until approximately 1890 when then Northwest

Territories Lieutenant Governor Dewdney set up a station on the Dominion Telegraph line. He called it Leduc to honour missionary Father Hippolyte Leduc of the Oblates of Mary Immaculate. Leduc was incorporated as a village in 1899 and a town in 1906.

The town's, province's, and country's future expanded when oil was first discovered at Leduc No. 1 on February 13, 1947. Leduc became a city on September 1, 1983, and today more than 20,000 residents live here. If you explore Leduc on foot or bicycle, you will find almost 38 kilometres of multi-use pathways winding through the city, including 10 kilometres of the Trans Canada Trail. A unique heritage site, the Stone Barn Garden is a pleasant stop when exploring the trails. Look for the barn in Leduc's Cultural Village on Telford Lake's south side, at 44th Street and 48th Avenue; it is located within William F. Lede Park. You will see a large timber-framed structure; its interior, though, has been re-created in stone to represent the original stone dairy barn that once stood on these grounds. Built with sections saved from the original barn's stone walls, the timber frame structure mimics a European post-and-beam construction model that is more than 600 years old.

Still popular with dairy farmers, Leduc County is called a "milkshed" because it is home to about 122 of Alberta's 1,422 dairy producers—almost 9 percent. It is also one of Alberta's top five regions for beef operations. Leduc holds an annual Canada Day celebration, followed by a berry festival in mid-July.

You will find a number of picnic spots including Telford Lake, Alexandra Park Ponds, Coady Lake, the Leduc Reservoir (good for trout fishing), and West Point Lake.

Leduc's visitor information centre is located at the chamber of commerce, at 6420–50th Street (780-986-5454).

Annual events include Leduc Black Gold Rodeo Days in early May, the Leduc West Antique Society–Country Swap Meet in late May, Alberta Dairy Congress in June, the Leduc West Exposition in July, Country Harvest in September, and the Santa Claus Parade and Festivities in late November.

Bringing in the sheaves at the Ukrainian Cultural Heritage Village (p. 55)

From top to bottom: A display of lanterns at *Luminaria* at the Devonian Botanic Garden (p. 91), Fort Assiniboine Museum (p. 34), and a stormy view of the Ribstones Historic Site (p. 99)

Clockwise from top left: Multicultural Heritage Centre in Stony Plain (p. 141), grain elevator in St. Albert (p. 9), and Sherwood Park Natural Area (p. 54)

JOAN MARIE GALAT

From top to bottom: Centennial Park in Edson (p. 162), Klondike Ferry (p. 31), and birdwatching viewpoint between Perryvale and Rochester (p. 36)

©ISTOCKPHOTO.COM/CREATIONS BY DAWN

ATHABASCA COUNTRY TOURISM

DAGMAR RAIS

©ISTOCKPHOTO.COM/NORTHERN PHOTO

From top to bottom: Grotto at Basilian Fathers Monastery in Mundare (p. 76), bison at Elk Island National Park (p. 56), and Fort Saskatchewan sheep and shepherd (p. 62)

CITY OF FORT SASKATCHEWAN

From top to bottom: Wetaskiwin City Hall reception area and former judges' chambers, opposite the courtroom (p. 111) and the Lacombe Corn Maze (p. 124)

Clockwise from top left:
The world's largest *pysanka*
at Vegreville (p. 78), Devon
Voyageur Park (p. 89),
and aerial view of Sherwood
Park (p. 51)

From top to bottom: The dried shores of Beaverhill Lake in Tofield (p. 104) and Astotin Lake in Elk Island National Park (p. 56)

Dr. Woods House Museum and Tea Room

Location: 4801–49th Avenue, Leduc.
Info: From the first Tuesday after the Canada Day (July 1) weekend to August 31, open Tuesday to Saturday, 11 a.m. to 5 p.m. Off-season hours are subject to change. Donations accepted. 780-986-1517.

There are few Western Canadian examples of a house that also served as a doctor's office. The Dr. Woods House Museum reflects rural Alberta life in the home where Dr. Woods lived and practised from 1927 until he died in 1936 at the age of 66. Restored to its original appearance, the distinctive bungalow includes original exhibits to showcase the doctor's medical practice. Monthly themed teas are held in the tea room, which is open during the same hours as the museum.

Pioneer Village Museum and Alberta Heritage Exposition Park

Location: 5 km west of Leduc on Hwy 39, and 1 km north on Range Road 260.
Info: 780-986-5912; www.leducwestantique.com/park.htm.

The Pioneer Village Museum and Alberta Heritage Exposition Park is on 32 hectares (80 acres) of land where historical buildings house antique equipment and displays. Be sure to visit the sawmill, blacksmith shop, and old smithy, as well as the Bellis & Morcom steam engine generator—driven by a piston steam engine made in 1927 in Birmingham, England.

Castrol Raceway

Location: Between Leduc and Edmonton, on the north side of the Edmonton Airport. Travel south on Hwy 2 and exit west onto Hwy 19 before Leduc.
Info: Seasons run May to October. 780-461-5801; 1-877-331-RACE (7223); Event hotline: 780-468-FAST (3278); www.castrolraceway.com.

Located next to the Edmonton airport, Castrol Raceway features a quarter-mile IHRA-sanctioned dragstrip, a ⅜-mile clay oval track, a 10-Acer Full Pro Motocross Track, and mini-sprint cart track. You will find grandstand viewing, concessions, and a playground for the kids.

Amazing Field Maze

Location: 10 minutes south of Leduc on Hwy 2A, and 1.5 km east on Township Road 484.
Info: Admission charged; groups of 11 or more who book in advance receive a 10 percent discount. 780-986-9034; www.amazingfieldmaze.ca.

As well as spending a couple of hours getting lost at the 4-hectare (10-acre) Amazing Field Maze, you can pet farm animals, play horseshoes and volleyball, and reserve the firepit for a wiener roast or evening by the fire. Be sure to wear sturdy shoes when planning to trek through a corn field.

DEVON

Directions: Exit Edmonton on Hwy 2 south, take Exit 525 to Hwy 19 west, stay right at the fork, and follow the signs to Devon, merging onto Hwy 19 and turning north at Hwy 60.
Distance: 41.2 km, or about 41 minutes, from Edmonton.
Info: 780-987-8300; www.town.devon.ab.ca.

Situated on the scenic banks of the North Saskatchewan River, Devon was established to accommodate the oil boom after the Imperial Oil discovery of the Leduc-Woodbend Oilfield. The famous Discovery Well is located 1 kilometre south of the town, which takes its name from the 1,500-metre (5,000-foot) underground strata called the Devonian rock formation.

Before Devon was established, people working for oil companies typically lived in two-room houses—skid shacks that could be loaded onto a trailer and moved from site to site. Needing houses and services for oil field workers, Imperial Oil purchased 49 hectares (120 acres) of barley fields, bordered on two sides by the North Saskatchewan River. House building started in January 1948, and 123 homes were occupied by the end of January the following year. Families moving to Devon were thrilled to have a home with at least three rooms—not to mention a foundation. Though most of these houses have been renovated, some original Esso homes can still be seen in Devon—a town now home to 6,361 residents.

Incorporated by 1950, Devon is called Canada's Model Town because it was the first community in Canada to be designed from scratch with the approval of a regional planning commission.

The town's location on the North Saskatchewan River provides a multitude of opportunities for independent exploration. A number of local businesses provide guided canoeing, jet skiing, and fishing opportunities. The beautiful river valley accommodates hiking, berry picking, wildlife viewing, fishing, boating, gold panning, and bird-watching, while cross-country ski trails in the Devon river valley will tempt skiers of all ages and abilities. Devon Days are held annually on the weekend after the Victoria Day weekend. Other annual events include the East of 60 Dinner Theatre in early March, International Women's Day, always on March 8, the 5 Peaks Trail Running Series, the Grand Prix of Cycling in June, the Devon Dust-up Cross Country Mountain Bike Race, Turkey Chase (Thanksgiving Monday), and Christmas in the Park (the last Saturday of November).

Canadian Petroleum Interpretive Centre—Leduc Oil Well No. 1 and Hall of Fame

Location: 50339–Hwy 60, 2 km south of Devon at the junction of Hwy 60 and Hwy 19.
Info: Open daily from 9 a.m. to 5 p.m. Admission charged. 780-987-4323; www.c-pic.org.

The Canadian Petroleum Discovery Centre at the Leduc No. 1 Historical Site recognizes struggles and triumphs in the Alberta oil patch. From 1912 to the time oil was discovered in Leduc, Imperial drilled 133 dry holes in a row. Toronto headquarters authorized workers to

Leduc Oil Well No. 1 and Canadian Petroleum Interpretive Centre near Devon

attempt a series of last-chance wells, and the Leduc well made history on February 13, 1947.

The Canadian Petroleum Discovery Centre showcases Canada's oil industry. Visitors can stand on the floor of a 1940s drilling rig and imagine the excitement when oil was discovered at this very spot, as well as browse artifacts, scale models, and indoor and outdoor interpretive displays that present the rich history and progress of Alberta's petroleum heritage.

Lions Campground (Pat O'Brien Memorial Park)

Location: From Hwy 60, turn into Devon at Athabasca Avenue; continue straight at the four-way stop; turn left onto Pidgeon Street, turn right onto Saskatchewan Avenue and continue downhill into the river valley to 1140 Saskatchewan Avenue east.
Info: Wheelchair accessible. $5 per car day-use fee, but free for Devon residents; 780-987-4777; www.devonlionspark.com.

Connected to the town of Devon, the Devon Lions Campground is a quiet river valley park on the banks of the North Saskatchewan River.

Devon Voyageur Park

The campground welcomes picnickers, and leashed pets are welcome. You will find numerous scenic trails, ideal for walking or biking, as well as a canoe launch, picnic tables, horseshoe pits, a playground, a ball field, washrooms, and a pet area. The park is used for a variety of special events including Devon Days, Sunday in the Park, the 5 Peaks Trail Running Series, and Christmas in the Park.

Devon Voyageur Park

Location: The end of Saskatchewan Avenue west, Devon.

Located along the North Saskatchewan River and visible from Highway 60, Devon Voyageur Park is a 16-hectare (40 acre) area linking more than 24 kilometres of natural and paved trails through the river valley and the Town of Devon. Opened in June 2006, the park has picnic tables, a boat launch, gazebo, and washroom facilities. Interpretive components that pertain to local flora and fauna, the Voyageurs, and other river history are being added.

Clifford E. Lee Nature Sanctuary

Location: 7 km north of Devon; go north on Hwy 60, turn left (west) on Woodbend Road, then turn left (south) on Sanctuary Road.
Info: Open year-round. Donations appreciated. Boardwalk and trails are easy for people of all skill levels to navigate. Limited wheelchair access can be arranged. 780-430-7134 or 780-987-4883; www.cliffordelee.com; info@cliffordelee.com.

The Clifford E. Lee Nature Sanctuary is a 141-hectare (348 acre) nature preserve of marshes, meadow, and pine and aspen woodland. It is a pleasant walk into the sanctuary on a boardwalk that leads to well-defined trails and sturdy viewing platforms on and near the water. More than 100 species of birds live here; spring and fall are the best times for observing. You are likely to see American coots, red-necked grebes, American bitterns, ruffed grouse, broad-winged hawks, and Canada geese—some using flax bale nesting platforms. Bird feeders at various locations bring songbirds quite close to viewing areas. (One mild February day during a walk along the Pine Knoll Trail, I had the pleasure of black-capped chickadees landing on my hand. The first one appeared uninvited, though it was much appreciated. Others came when I held out a few sunflower seeds from one of the feeders. Perhaps they become tame as a result of frequent visitors to the area.)

Those who enjoy wildflowers will especially take pleasure in the sanctuary from May through August. Look for my favourite early June bloomers: lily-of-the-valley and wintergreen. Be sure, also, to watch for the yellow petals of flowering lady's slippers along the meadow's border around the Father's Day weekend. Many other species bloom in July, with the showy fringed gentians and evening primrose appearing in both July and August.

Shalom Park

Location: Exit Edmonton on Hwy 2 south and turn west onto Ellerslie Road (9th Avenue SW); turn south on 170th Street/Range Road 253, drive 4 km, and turn west at the T-intersection onto Township Road 510 and follow to Shalom Park.

Info: Except during special events, the gate is always closed. Push the call button to gain access. 780-955-3503; www.shalompark.com.

Recognized as one of the top ten water-skiing facilities in the world, Shalom Park is a constructed lake in the natural landscape of the North Saskatchewan River valley. The park is owned by Ken Nelson, a national champion who has set several national records. Many of the most prestigious national and international tournaments have been held here. Even if you do not ski, a visit to Shalom Park will provide a pleasant picnic site with some potentially spectacular water-skiing entertainment, especially during tournaments. You will find a large deck with tables and chairs and lots of room on the dock. You do not have to be club member to visit, and you can even ski or ask to ride in a tow boat for a closer look at the sport.

Edmonton Corn Maze

Location: 1.6 km (1 mile) east of Hwy 60 on Hwy 627. Exit Edmonton on Whitemud Drive West, turn left at 215 Street/Winterburn Road NW, and turn right at Hwy 627.
Info: Admission charged. 780-288-0208 or 780-554-4540; www.edmontoncorn maze.ca; edmontoncornmaze@gmail.com.

On 4 hectares (10 acres), the Edmonton Corn Maze sports a new and challenging design each year. The course will take 30 minutes if you make all the right turns, but it is more likely to require about an hour to find your way through more than 5 kilometres of twists and turns and 85 decision points. You can also enjoy pedal carts, farm animals, a bale mountain, and a picnic area. Be sure to wear sturdy shoes when planning to trek through a corn maze.

Devonian Botanic Garden

Location: Exit Edmonton on Whitemud Drive West, turn left at 215 Street/ Winterburn Road NW, turn right at Hwy 627/Township Road 520, turn left at Hwy 60 South, and turn left at Clymont Road/Township Road 514A.
Info: Open daily from April until the first snowfall or through Thanksgiving. Hours

may fluctuate. Admission charged. Tram tours may be limited or unavailable during special events. 780-987-3054; www.devonian.ualberta.ca.

Established in 1959 by the University of Alberta, the Devonian Botanic Garden is the northernmost botanic garden in Canada. Give yourself lots of time to visit its 32 hectares (80 acres) of gardens and 45 hectares (110 acres) of natural area, and ask the gate attendant what is special to see on the day you visit. The gardens are set in rolling landscape, alongside pine trees and large ponds. Outdoor pathways lead through spectacular flower gardens, native and alpine plants, and ecological reserves. This is a great place to familiarize yourself with the names of flora that are local and introduced, especially if you visit throughout the summer so you can see how plants look during each stage of their growth. Make sure you do not miss the tranquil Kurimoto Japanese Garden, which is designed to encourage meditation and reflection.

A walk through the butterfly house offers a wondrous experience, as colourful wings flutter and soar overhead—sometimes alighting close enough to be photographed. Wear a loud Hawaiian shirt or something with a floral print if you want them to land on you!

CAMROSE

Directions: Exit Edmonton on Hwy 16 east, take the Anthony Henday Drive exit onto Hwy 216 south toward Hwy 14 east, exit onto Hwy 14 east, merge onto Hwy 21/Range Road 230. Follow Hwy 21 and turn left at Hwy 623/Township Road 494; continue to follow Hwy 623; take a slight right at Hwy 833, and turn left at Hwy 617, then right at Hwy 833.
Distance: 104 km, or about 1 hour and 19 minutes, from Edmonton.
Info: www.tourismcamrose.com.

The Camrose city centre surrounds picturesque Mirror Lake, which flows from Stoney Creek and forms the central point of the city's urban parks. A flock of trumpeter and Polish mute swans live at the lake in summer and spend their winters at a city facility. Paralleled by paved walking paths, Stoney Creek meanders through the city's grassy river valley.

Originally the hamlet of Stoney Creek, present-day Camrose was first named after Reverend Dr. Sparling of Winnipeg and incorporated as the village of Sparling. To avoid confusion with Sperling, Manitoba, and Stirling, Alberta, its name was changed again when its first post office opened. "Camrose" was likely chosen from the 1905 British postal guide and named after a community in South Wales.

Before European settlement, the Camrose region was home to the Cree First Nation. In the 1750s, Anthony Henday probably became the first European to travel here when he followed the Battle River valley from the east—a route the first homesteaders later used. In the early 1900s, most immigrants who settled in the Camrose area came from Scandinavian countries, like Norway and Sweden, but many also arrived from the United States.

In 1904, Duncan Sampson built Camrose's first commercial building, using a wagonload of lumber hauled from Wetaskiwin. You can see its restored incarnation at the corner of 50th Street and 50th Avenue. The Camrose Main Street Project has involved enhancing nearly 20 of the more than 50 downtown buildings that are over 50 years old. You can take a self-guided historic walking tour. A brochure is available at the tourist information centre—Camrose Main Street Project office (4949–50th Street), and online at www.downtowncamrose.com.

Camrose was proclaimed a city on January 1, 1955, and today about 16,000 people live here. You may want to time your visit to coincide with an event such as Artsfest, National Aboriginal Day celebrations, Jaywalkers Jamboree, the Big Valley Jamboree, Camrose Founders Days, Canada Day celebrations, or Music in the Park (each Thursday night from late June until the end of August).

Mirror Lake Park, Tourist Information Centre, and Bill Fowler Centre

Location: 5402–48th Avenue, Camrose.
Info: 780-672-4217.

Visible from Highway 13, the Camrose tourist information centre is located at the Bill Fowler Centre. You can see a half-scale replica of a Viking longship, interpretive panels that describe park features and city history, and a nature mural carved out of red brick. Paved and lit walking paths encircle Mirror Lake and lead to various picnic sites with washrooms.

Camrose & District Centennial Museum

Location: 4522–53rd Street, Camrose.
Info: Open from the Victoria Day weekend to the Labour Day weekend, Tuesday to Sunday, 10 a.m. to 5 p.m.; by appointment during the rest of the year. Donations appreciated. 780-672-3298; www.camrosemuseum.ca.

The Camrose & District Centennial Museum displays clothing, musical instruments, and other artifacts in a variety of refurbished and reconstructed buildings. You can visit the newspaper office, fire hall, RCMP station, machine building, blacksmith shop, Oldtimers Hut, Mona Sparling Building, Likeness School, St. Dunstan's Church, and Pioneer Home. The textiles collection comprises nearly 3,000 artifacts that originate from between 1860 and 1960. Numerous photos, a 1912 steam engine, and a fascinating replica of a log and sod home depict local history.

Camrose Railway Station and Freight Shed Tea Room

Location: 4407–47th Avenue, Camrose.
Info: The Camrose Railway Station is open from the Victoria Day weekend to the Labour Day weekend, 10 a.m. to 5 p.m.; or by appointment year-round. The Freight Shed Tea Room is open Thursday and Friday from 1 p.m. to 5 p.m., and Saturdays from 10 a.m. to 5 p.m. 780-672-3099; northernsociety@incentre.net.

The Camrose Railway Station and Tea Room are part of the park system and are in the centre of Camrose's heritage district. The 1911 Canadian Northern Railway station contains a distinctive collection of local railway history and includes a G-Scale Garden Railway with model historic buildings and gardens. There is also a large wooden creative play train.

Alberta's Littlest Airport

Location: About 25 km from Camrose; drive 22 km east on Hwy 13, turn south on Kelsey Road, and travel approximately 4 km to the field entrance on the road's west side.
Info: www.camrosemodellers.ca.

Located near the village of Bawlf, Alberta's Littlest Airport features five runways where model aircraft operators gather to fly planes and race cars. The airport includes a firepit, play area, frequency building, model race car and aircraft hanger, hobby shop, and washroom facilities, including a wheelchair-accessible washroom. Four major events are hosted during the year, but any weekend offers the probability of seeing aviators and drivers in action.

Tillicum Beach Park at Dried Meat Lake

Location: About 1 km east of Camrose and 14 km south of Hwy 13. Exit Camrose on Hwy 13 (east) and turn right on the newly paved Dried Meat Lake Road. Follow the signs.
Info: Open May to September. Tillicum Beach Park Office: 780-672-6880. County of Camrose: 780-672-4446.

A long, narrow lake encompassing 16.5 square kilometres, Dried Meat Lake formed above a natural constriction of the Battle River in a glacial meltwater channel that cuts 40 metres into the surrounding prairie. Dried Meat Lake and Dried Meat Hill, just east of the lake's centre, take their names from the Cree, who dried bison meat and mixed it with saskatoon berries to make pemmican. Members of the Cree tribe traditionally lived east of the Battle River, while the Blackfoot remained west of the river. The river defined their territories and was the location of many clashes between the tribes, giving rise to the waterway's name.

The stunning lake view from the top of the valley makes it easy to imagine the lake's role as an important transportation route, especially when the roads turned to mud every spring. In the early 1900s, settlers who came to farm the area's rich soil were ferried across the lake on a 9-metre boat with a wood-burning steam engine.

Stabilized by a weir, the lake has a maximum depth of 3.7 metres and offers canoeing, kayaking, motor boating, fishing, wildlife viewing, and swimming. Located on the lake's eastern shore, Tillicum Beach Park has a day-use area, beach, playground, ball diamonds, firepits, fish cleaning stand, picnic shelter, flush toilets, concession, and boat launch. You can also launch small boats on the lake's south end, near the weir, where Highway 56 crosses the Battle River.

MIQUELON LAKE PROVINCIAL PARK

Directions: Exit Edmonton on Hwy 16 east, and take Anthony Henday Drive NW/Hwy 216 south toward Hwy 14 east; continue on Hwy 14 to the Camrose ramp and merge south onto Hwy 21/Range Road 230; turn left at Hwy 623/Township Road 494, and take a slight right at Hwy 833.
Distance: 74.9 km, or about 56 minutes, from Edmonton.
Info: Boat launches may be closed to powerboats when water levels are low, but a hand launch is available for canoes and other small craft. All boats are prohibited from entering certain waterfowl nesting areas and places along the beach. Firewood is sold at the store by the park's front entrance. 780-672-7308.

Situated on the southern edge of the Cooking Lake Moraine, Miquelon Lake Provincial Park is dominated by white-spruce forests, as well as the trembling aspen and balsam poplar that define the northern portion of Alberta's aspen parkland belt. Numerous ponds and wetlands mark the park's 1,299 hectares (3,210 acres). Wild rose, saskatoon, raspberry, buffalo berry, pin cherry, and dogwood are just some of the plants that provide habitat for the more than 200 bird species found here.

Shallow and salty, Miquelon Lake is a recognized Important Bird Area and a good place to see species that prefer older woodland—western wood-pewees, ovenbirds, yellow warblers, northern orioles, and rose-breasted grosbeaks. Sora, green-winged teals, American coots, and ruddy ducks seek the park's marsh areas, while great flocks of California and ring-billed gulls nest on Gull Island, colonizing by the thousands. Ducks and shorebirds, including sanderlings and red-necked phalaropes, use the lake during spring and fall migration.

The park's day-use area has change rooms, firepits, horseshoe pitches, picnic shelters, and flush toilets, as well as an amphitheatre and visitor centre. A trail system, with loops ranging in length from 1.7 to 10 kilometres, winds through the park's knob and kettle terrain. The loops provide opportunities for hiking, cycling, and nature exploration. Stop at the visitor centre to find out about guided hikes and other programs. Summertime visitors can enjoy canoeing, kayaking, hiking, sailing, swimming, and windsurfing. The saline water helps inhibit algae growth, and the lake is often quite clear.

Winter visitors can enjoy ice skating on a flooded area and 18 kilometres of groomed cross-country ski trails.

VIKING

Directions: Exit Edmonton on Hwy 16 east, take Anthony Henday Drive NW/Hwy 216 south toward Hwy 14 east; continue on Hwy 14 east, turn left at Hwy 36, and turn right at 51st Avenue.
Distance: 142 km, or about 1 hour and 46 minutes, from Edmonton.
Info: 780-336-2544; www.town.viking.ab.ca.

Early Norwegian settlers named Viking after their pirating ancestors. The first post office opened in July 1904, but town incorporation did not follow until 1952. Today Viking is home to almost 1,100 people. You will find the Viking Station Gallery and Arts Centre Guild (5001–51st Avenue) houses a tearoom and gallery with local artists' work in a converted CN Station. Beside the CN Station, Viking Troll

Viking ship head at Viking Hill Park

Park has a Scandinavian theme—with trolls populating the park and trees. You can enjoy a picnic, count all the trolls you can find, and see a Viking ship guarded by a Viking warrior.

National Hockey League fans will know Viking as the *Home of the Sutters*—six brothers who learned to play hockey here and achieved National Hockey League fame. They played a total of 4,994 regular season games and 603 playoff games, scoring 1,320 goals and 1,615 assists.

Viking Historical Museum

Location: 5108–61st Avenue, Viking.
Info: Open from the Victoria Day weekend until late summer, Wednesday to Friday, 10 a.m. to 5 p.m., and by appointment during the off-season. Guided tours are available upon request. Donations welcome. Buildings are wheelchair accessible, but washrooms are not. 780-336-3066.

The Viking Historical Museum depicts the lives of the area's first Scandinavian settlers. Pioneer theme rooms show how the community

View from Ribstones Historic Site in Viking

changed from its early agricultural base due to oil and gas development. The Viking Municipal Hospital, built in 1921, was converted to house the museum in 1984. A pioneer village on the site includes a 1907 school, a 1903 log store, a 1919 farmhouse, and a 1938 church. The museum has a spot for picnicking.

Ribstones Historic Site

Location: About 13 km from Viking. Exit Viking on Hwy 14 east, drive 11 km then watch the road's south side for a sign describing the ribstones. About 50 metres east of the sign, turn south onto Range Road 120, which leads to a T-junction after about 1.5 km. Turn left and—almost immediately—right, and follow the markers to the Ribstones on Range Road 120.

Info: Located on private land. Admission is free. The site is revered by Aboriginal peoples and should be treated with respect. Do not disturb braids of sweetgrass placed on the stones, or prayer flags hanging in nearby trees.

The Ribstones are a set of quartzite boulders known as glacial erratics—stones carried many thousands of kilometres by great continental

Quarzite boulder known as a ribstone

glaciers. The rocks carved into the Ribstones came from the Canadian Shield, and some weigh more than a ton. Aboriginal people chiselled symbols into the rock—petroglyphs that are now at least 1,000 years old. One of only nine sets found in Alberta, the Viking ribstones are especially revered as a grouping that can be seen at its original location atop a hill in the rolling land near Viking.

Long, parallel grooves etched into the stones are believed to represent a bison's rib cage. The pale stones were likely used in bison fertility ceremonies to encourage the appearance of large bison herds. Rituals included leaving gifts on the stones to ensure a good hunt or as thanks for successful hunting.

TOFIELD

Directions: Exit Edmonton on Hwy 16 east, take Anthony Henday Drive NW/Hwy 216 south toward Hwy 14 east, and continue on Hwy 14 to Tofield.

Distance: About 57 km southeast from Edmonton.
Info: 780-662-3269; www.tofieldalberta.ca.

Pioneers began arriving in this area around 1886, travelling by cart on old bison trails. The community was named after Dr. J. A. Tofield, an early settler who served in the Riel Rebellion as an army doctor. Born in Yorkshire, England, Tofield was educated as a doctor and engineer at Oxford.

To send and receive mail, early pioneers had to wait until someone happened to ride the trail between Tofield and Edmonton. When the post office opened in 1898, Tofield's first postmaster earned $12 for his first year of service—and sold $36 in stamps.

In 1909, Tofield became an incorporated town and acquired its first telephone, providing service from 8 a.m. to 8 p.m. on weekdays, and 8 a.m. to 4 p.m. on Sundays.

When the Grand Trunk Pacific Railroad proposed its route through Tofield, the town moved to a new northwest site. Unfortunately, the railroad changed its route, and the town moved again to what is its current location. Residents finally welcomed the railway in 1909.

In 1910, the town drilled for water but discovered natural gas. A temporary boom marked by skyrocketing land prices came to pass, and for a few short years Tofield was enthusiastically dubbed the "Hamilton of the west." The boom died by 1913, and subdivisions meant for housing became farmland. The town survived thanks to the railway and its coal industry, comprising two strip mines and one underground mine. At its peak, Tofield Coal employed 100 men and shipped more than 180,000 tons of coal a year.

Now home to almost 2,000 people, Tofield is perhaps best known for its proximity to the large and shallow Beaverhill Lake situated 8 kilometres east. Beaverhill Lake is a collection basin for runoff from the Beaver Hills, which are from 60 to 120 metres higher than the surrounding land. The hills were created when the Keewatin glacier deposited the debris and boulders that form the hills' knob and kettle landscape. Before European settlers came to the area, Aboriginals lived and hunted in the Beaver Hills, a region rich with bison, bear, moose, deer, and beaver, as well as the thousands of waterfowl drawn to Beaverhill Lake.

Between 2 and 3 metres deep, the 161- by 10-kilometre lake is a waterfowl staging spot and an internationally recognized Important Bird Area of Global Significance. It welcomes tens of thousands of migrating birds who rest and feed here before returning to their flight paths. More than 270 bird species have been identified here, including 40 different shorebird species that frequent the lakes' southern end.

The lake serves more than 1 percent of the world's population of greater white-fronted geese, snow geese, pectoral sandpipers, black-bellied sandpipers, and dowitcher species, as well as more than 1 percent of the national population of American Avocets, which breed here. Piping plovers, an endangered species, have also bred at Beaverhill Lake. A staging area, the lake allows snow geese and greater white-fronted geese to build fat reserves in preparation for the incubation period and migration.

Canada geese return in March, with greater white-fronted geese, snow geese, tundra swans, and numerous duck species following on their tail feathers. Rough-legged and red-tailed hawks, bald eagles, merlins, northern harriers, and northern goshawks arrive next. Peregrine falcons usually pass through between mid- and late April, on their way to more northerly destinations.

Beaverhill Bird Observatory

Location: About 75 km from Edmonton—a 50-minute drive and 20-minute walk to the observatory. Exit Edmonton on Hwy 14 east to Tofield. You can take the route through town by following the Watchable Wildlife signs, or stay on Hwy 14, turning north at Secondary Hwy 834.

- Go north until you reach a T-intersection.
- At the T-intersection, turn right (east) onto Rowan's Route.
- Follow Rowan's Route almost to the end, and go through the swing gate on the left.
- Drive through this gate (closing the gate behind you) and proceed to a second gate.

- Park your vehicle inside the second gate to prevent cattle from scratching against your car.
- Walk east along the trail and follow the signs to the observatory.

Info: Rowan's Route can get slippery when wet. For information, visit www.beaver hillbirds.com or www.bsc-eoc.org.

The Beaverhill Bird Observatory monitors bird migration almost every day in May and August. Birds are captured using mist nets and brought to the lab for identification, ageing, sexing, and banding. Between 2,000 and 4,500 birds are banded every year, and visitors may watch bird-banding operations in the mornings.

Located at the southeast corner of the lake, the observatory provides tours in spring and summer. Directional signage and a kiosk at the main parking area will lead you to excellent water bird, songbird, and raptor viewing opportunities.

The observatory maintains and monitors tree swallow boxes along the lake's south shore and organizes nocturnal owl surveys and other events, such as the annual Baillie Birdathon, which involves a fun day of identifying as many species as possible during a 24-hour period.

LISA PRIESTLEY

Mountain bluebird—a common sight in and around the Beaverhill Lake Natural Area

The annual Birding Breakfast at the end of May provides an opportunity to observe banding operations.

Beaverhill Lake Nature Centre and Tofield Museum

Location: 5028–48th Avenue, Tofield. Exit Hwy 14 and take the access road to Tofield; look for a tower with birdhouses.
Info: Summer hours are Tuesday to Saturday from 10 a.m. to 6 p.m., Sundays from 2 p.m. to 4 p.m. For winter hours (from October through April), call the Tofield town office at 780-662-3269 to arrange a visit or 780-662-3191 for a museum tour. The nature centre is closed in winter. www.tofieldalberta.ca/nature.htm.

The Beaverhill Lake Nature Centre offers wildlife interpretive displays, tourist information, and a unique gift shop containing bird feeders, books, and works by local crafters. The building also houses the Tofield Museum, which depicts the lives of early Aboriginal people and European settlers, as well as life in succeeding years. Displays encompass medicine, education, pioneer tools, everyday living, and early businesses. Artifacts are rotated to provide an ongoing variety of displays. You can view the art gallery displaying the work of local artists and take a self-guided walk at Nature's Marsh, a small natural area behind the centre. The Tofield historical walk includes buildings from the early 1900s, such as the Tofield Hotel and Dr. Bain's house. Tofield's oldest building is a Presbyterian Church built in 1904. The walk can take from 45 minutes to 2 hours, depending on how long you linger along the way. Ask for the historical walk brochure at the Nature Centre/Museum or town office.

MILLET

Directions: Exit Edmonton on Hwy 2 (south); take exit S16 to reach Hwy 2A toward Wetaskiwin, which becomes Hwy 616 into Millet.
Distance: 54 km, or about 48 minutes, from Edmonton.
Info: 780-387-4554; www.millet.ca.

Beaverhill Lake and Lister Lake weir

Millet calls itself Alberta's prettiest little town—a reasonable claim, considering the town is centred on a 26-hectare (65 acre) park system. Check out the Pipestone Creek Park with paved and lit pathways, trails, and the 24.6 by 14.4-metre Splash Pad at 4904–52nd Street.

The community was named in 1891 when Canadian Pacific Railway president Sir William Van Horne asked Father Lacombe to name the stations north of Lacombe on the new Calgary–Edmonton line. The missionary named the town after August Millet, his canoeman and one of his travelling companions.

The Millet walking tour passes a number of murals and historic points, some with plaques that detail each site's significance. You can pick up a walking tour brochure at the starting point—the Millet & District Museum & Archives & Visitor Information Centre (see page 107 for more on the museum). Walking the entire route takes about 1½ hours. Other than Pipestone Park's gentle hills, most of the tour follows flat terrain on sidewalks or paved paths; however, the walk does follow some shale pathways. You can reach main tour sections by vehicle. Low areas of the Pipestone Trail may be flooded after heavy rain.

There are a number of places to enjoy a picnic, including the gazebo at the Millet Memory Rose Garden (Highway 2A and 51st Avenue). The garden contains a myriad of rose species and colours; each plant has been purchased in memory of a loved one. The 2.4-hectare (6-acre) William Leonard Gray Park on Diamond Drive has playground equipment. The Burn's Creamery Garden is a heritage site with a plaque that tells the story of the creamery and its garden (situated along Highway 2A between 51st and 53rd avenues).

Along Highway 2A and 53rd Avenue, Millet's north end is home to the Bell Kiosk Garden, which contains the town's first school bell. Discover the story of the school, and see a mural of the school's interior while enjoying the scent and beauty of flowers and shrubs surrounded by grassy areas and tall trees. You will find a park bench and picnic table there. The Railway Station Garden (Highway 2A, on the east side of a truck parking area, and 49th Avenue) marks the original Canadian Pacific Railway Station location in Millet. A sign tells the story of

TRACEY LEAVITT

Mural on Millet Community Hall

the railway between Edmonton and Calgary, while the shrub garden enhances the spot with its colourful plant display. The Irish Garden (5148–50th Avenue) honours Millet's international partnership with Warringstown, Northern Ireland. Its shamrock design includes a rainbow-shaped planter in the centre, with a pot of gold (marigolds) at the base. The Trans Canada Trail/Legacy Garden is located on Highway 2A, where the trail crosses the railway. The V-shaped garden contains two cedar-lattice arched seats, shrubs, and perennials. The garden was established to celebrate two circumstances: Millet's Communities In Bloom partnership with Audley, England, and the moment cyclists carried a bottle of water through Millet on a trek between three oceans—the Arctic Ocean in Tuktoyuktuk, NWT, the Pacific Ocean at Victoria, BC, and the Atlantic Ocean at St. John's, NL.

Annual events include Millet Days, Millet Community Garage Sale, Garden Tour and Strawberry Tea, Country Gospel Concert, and Volksmarch.

Millet & District Museum & Archives & Visitor Information Centre

Location: 5120–50th Street, on the west side of Hwy 2A at Millet's north end.
Info: Open Victoria Day through Labour Day, Monday to Saturday, 8:30 a.m. to 4:30 p.m.; in winter, Tuesday, Wednesday, and Thursday, 1 p.m. to 3:30 p.m. Also open by appointment. General admission by donation, with admission charged for special events and group tours. Wheelchair accessible. 780-387-5558; www.milletmuseum.ca.

The Millet & District Museum has a collection of more than 5,000 artifacts from the first half of the 20th century, as well as an exhibit depicting Millet between 1891 and 1940 by way of four facades—the Millet Hotel, Burn Creamery, Livery Barn, and Mercantile Store. Room displays include the one-room Hillside School, Tool Shed, John Barth's Barbershop, and Kenny Kerr's Implement Office, as well as a bedroom, living room, and kitchen representative of periods between 1900 and 1950. Upstairs, the Veterans' Wall displays portraits of more than 200 Millet & District World War I and II veterans.

WETASKIWIN

Directions: Exit Edmonton on Hwy 2 south; take Exit 516 to reach Hwy 2A south to Wetaskiwin.
Distance: 71.2 km, or about 1 hour and 7 minutes, from Edmonton.
Info: 780-361-4417 or 1-800-989-6899; www.wetaskiwin.ca.

As with most Alberta communities, the first Europeans to visit and settle in the area were missionaries and government agents. But long before the settlers arrived, two Aboriginal tribes fought to protect their territories from each other. Hostile enemies, the Cree lived north and the Blackfoot lived south of the Red Deer River—a line that defined their hunting grounds. Every summer, Blackfoot warriors crossed the river to follow bison herds migrating north, sparking fierce battles and constant war.

According to legend, in about 1867 both tribes had young chiefs who had not yet fought each other. Planning a surprise attack, Chief Buffalo Child took his rifle and left to discover where the Cree were positioned. He travelled to the low hills north and west of present-day Wetaskiwin in search of a better view of the terrain and the Cree camps.

Also anxious to determine the enemy's location, Cree Chief Little Bear took his knife and made his way to the hills. Discovering each other face to face on the same knoll, the two chiefs put down their weapons and attacked each other with bared fists. Of equal size and strength, they tumbled, wrestled, and fought, but neither could overcome the other. Nearing exhaustion, they finally pulled away from each other to rest.

Watching Little Bear warily, Buffalo Child took out his pipe and began to smoke. Keeping his eyes on the Blackfoot warrior, Little Bear reached for his pipe but discovered it had broken during the struggle. Perhaps without thinking, the Blackfoot offered his pipe to the Cree, who automatically took the pipe and inhaled its rich flavour.

Tradition dictated that those who smoked from a shared pipe forged an unbreakable bond—a promise of peace and comradery.

Wetaskiwin water tower

The young chiefs returned to their tribes to tell the elders what they had done, then brought their tribes to the hill, where the peace pipe was passed and promises made to remain friends for all time. The hills became known as *Wee-Tas-Ki-Win-Spatinow*, which means "the hills where peace was made."

Historic 1907 courtroom inside Wetaskiwin City Hall

Still, peace did not reign everywhere. During the 1885 Northwest Rebellion, Fort Ethier was built to protect the Calgary–Edmonton Trail and provide a haven for settlers in the Wetaskiwin area. You can still see the log block building at its original location, although it is not accessible.

In 1890, work started on the C&E Railway between Calgary and Edmonton. During construction, Wetaskiwin was called Siding 16— the 16th stop in the line north from Calgary. Sidings were spaced every 7 or 8 miles to allow trains travelling in opposite directions to meet one another. When this northern point was reached in 1891, settlers built a community around the train station. The following year, Father Lacombe suggested that Siding 16 be called Wetaskiwin. The community incorporated as a town in 1902 and became Canada's smallest city in 1906.

A terrible fire destroyed much of Wetaskiwin's wood-framed downtown in 1903. New businesses made of brick, sandstone, and tyndal stone sprang up. You can follow interpretive signs through Wetaskiwin's historic downtown and see several early-20th-century buildings—a number of which feature murals depicting local history. For those who like to shop along a main street, Wetaskiwin's historical downtown core is also the place to browse through antique stores, gift and fashion boutiques, and galleries. For a longer walk, explore the town's beautiful walking trails connecting the downtown, Auto Mile, By-the-Lake Park, and Reynolds Alberta Museum. Directional brochures are available at the Wetaskiwin & District Chamber of Commerce Visitor Information Centre (4910–55A Street) on the Auto Mile, on Highway 2A through Wetaskiwin. Home to more than 12,000 people, the city of Wetaskiwin has the highest per capita auto sales in the country and is called the Car Capital of Canada because of the multitude of vehicle dealerships on the Wetaskiwin Auto Mile.

There are two landmarks to note at the east and west entrances of the downtown core. Erected in 1906, the oldest working water tower in Canada can be seen as you enter the city from any direction. It is located at the west entrance—Highway 2A and 50th Street. Look for the restored 1907 courthouse, now Wetaskiwin City Hall, at the city's east entrance—47th Street and 50th Avenue. Be sure to inspect this national historic building's carved ionic columns and elaborate cornice work—common features of its modern renaissance style. Guided tours of the old courthouse/new city hall are available on Wednesdays, from May through September. During the rest of the year, visitors can take a self-guided tour through the building. Annual events include the Harvest Festival, and Gingerbread and Glitter.

Wetaskiwin & District Heritage Museum

Location: 5007–50th Avenue, Wetaskiwin.
Info: Open from the Saturday of the Victoria Day weekend through to the end of September, Tuesday to Saturday, 10 a.m. to 5 p.m.; open the rest of the year, 10 a.m. to 5 p.m. from Tuesday to Friday, and 10 a.m. to 4 p.m. on Saturday. Closed Sunday and Monday. Admission by donation. Wheelchair accessible. 780-352-0227; www.wetaskiwinmuseum.com.

Located on Wetaskiwin's main street, the Wetaskiwin & District Museum has three floors of exhibits that expand on the fur trade, fur farming, and Aboriginal history, as well as Hutterite and Chinese immigration. Activities and changing exhibits make subsequent visits new experiences. Don't miss the Children's Legacy Centre or general store, hotel room, and garage re-creations, as well as opportunities to enjoy special events during Canada Day and Pioneer Days.

Reynolds-Alberta Museum and Canada's Aviation Hall of Fame

Location: 2 km west of Wetaskiwin on Hwy 13.
Info: Open daily during peak season (mid-May through September), 10 a.m. to 5 p.m., until 6 p.m. in July and August; off-season (September to mid-May), 10 a.m. to 5 p.m. Closed Mondays. Phone for season dates. Admission charged. 780-361-1351; www.cahf.ca and www.machinemuseum.net.

The Reynolds-Alberta Museum reveals Alberta's mechanical history with more than 8,000 artifacts that focus on transportation, agriculture, aviation, and industry. Exhibits display vehicles, aircraft, tractors, and other industrial machines. Many rare and irreplaceable artifacts date from as early as the 1880s. You can enjoy hands-on activities, demonstrations, audio-visual shows, interpreter-led programs, and seasonal special events.

Look for Canada's Aviation Hall of Fame next to the Reynolds-Alberta Museum.

This is the country's only aviation museum devoted to preserving accounts of the more than 150 inducted members who have contributed to Canada's distinguished aviation history.

Alberta Central Railway Museum

Location: About 14 km southeast of Wetaskiwin. Follow signs on Hwy 2A, Hwy 13, and at each turn. Look for the grain elevator.
Info: Open from the Victoria Day weekend to the Labour Day weekend, Wednesday to Sunday and holiday Mondays, 10 a.m. to 4 p.m. Admission charged. Trains usually run at 1:30 p.m. and 3 p.m. Call 780-352-2257 to confirm train schedule as very occasionally trains do not run; www.abcentralrailway.com.

Stock-car racer at Edmonton International Raceway

The Alberta Central Railway Museum offers visitors a step-back-in-time experience. A visit to the 1907 Wetaskiwin CPR depot replica reveals a typical country station, complete with a waiting room, baggage room, and telegraph office. This is your chance to enjoy lunch in a 1920 café car and take a train ride. You can see how a semaphore was used to control train movements, and view the collection of Canadian Pacific rolling stock, maintenance-of-way tools, and track motor cars. The museum's 1959 RS23 locomotive ex-CP 8015 was used for passenger service and is Canada's only preserved Montreal Locomotive Works Alco design lightweight locomotive.

Alberta's second-oldest standing grain elevator, built in 1906 by the Alberta Grain Company, was added to the museum in 2002. It provides a unique opportunity to see how railways and elevators were used together.

Edmonton International Raceway

Location: 4 km west of the junction of Hwy 13 and Hwy 2A in Wetaskiwin.
Info: Races take place on Saturday nights from early May through early October. 780-352-8054; event hotline: 780-467-9276; www.edmontonraceway.com.

The Edmonton International Raceway offers family entertainment on north-central Alberta's only paved oval stock-car racetrack. Sanctioned by NASCAR, IMCA Canada, INEX (Legend Cars), and the Baby Grand Stock Car Association, it has one of the highest numbers of race cars at events in the region, in all its race classes. This 0.4-kilometre (¼-mile) paved oval features a wide variety of race classes, including entry-level Feature Stocks to high-end NASCAR Late Models. Other popular events include Hit to Pass and Super Motard Motorcycle Racing. Activities geared to children encompass junior race-fan draws, driver autograph sessions, race car rides, Frisbee toss, and birthday parties.

RED DEER

Directions: Exit Edmonton on Hwy 2 south.
Distance: 157 km, or about 1 hour and 42 minutes, from Edmonton.
Info: 403-342-8111; www.city.red-deer.ab.ca.

The Red Deer region is a transition zone between the moister aspen parkland and the drier prairie. Blackfoot, Plains Cree, and Stoney Aboriginal tribes lived here before Métis, fur traders, and European settlers came to the area. Local riverbanks teemed with elk, and the Cree named the river *Waskasoo seepee*, meaning "Elk River." Mistaking the elk for a type of European red deer, early British fur traders misinterpreted the name to mean Red Deer River.

Many people travelled through Red Deer on trips between Calgary and Edmonton. As the bison neared extinction, farmers came to the area to grow grain, set up ranches, and establish dairy farms. Eventually they heard talk of a railway that would join Edmonton and Calgary, and surveyors came looking for the least expensive place to bridge the Red Deer River. Farmer and speculator Reverend Leonard Gaetz directed them to a spot along his land—offering the Calgary and Edmonton Railway a half-share of about 502 hectares (1,240 acres) of his own land to develop as a townsite. They agreed and the first train to travel from Calgary to Edmonton passed through Red Deer in 1891.

By 1901, Red Deer incorporated as a town of 323 residents. Settlers surged here, and Red Deer incorporated as a city of 2,800 people in 1913, but the boom ended with World War I. After World War II, oil and natural gas discoveries boosted growth, and by the late 1950s Red Deer was calling itself Canada's fastest-growing city. Today it is Alberta's third-largest city and home to more than 87,000 residents.

Get a feel for the community by strolling through Red Deer's downtown. Include a visit to City Hall Park and check out one of Canada's largest bronze sculpture collections. Outdoor statues and other art honour the characters and events that shaped Red Deer history. These sculptures can be found downtown, along the trails, at Red Deer College, and on Alexander Way. You will also find artwork by local, national, and international artists at the Red Deer Museum and Art Gallery, Red Deer College, Allied Arts Council, the Red Deer Public Library's Kiwanis Gallery, and Harris-Warke Gallery.

In addition to numerous summer festivals, annual Red Deer events include the Agricultural Showcase of Alberta—Agri-Trade Exhibition with exhibitors from Canada and international locations. Red Deer's annual summer fair is called Westerner Days.

Consider taking one of Red Deer's most interesting walking tours. The Ghost Tour illuminates stories about eight different ghosts as well as the legend of a pig on the lam. Tours also take in three murals and various historic buildings and sites. St. Mary's Church, completed in 1968, is an early work of architect Douglas Cardinal. Visit www .downtownreddeer.com or the Red Deer Museum and Art Gallery for self-guided ghost and mural walking tour information.

South of 43rd Street and next to the Red Deer Arena, the Red Deer Public Market includes buskers, musicians, and a wide variety of vendors from across Alberta, as well fruit sellers from British Columbia. It opens on the Victoria Day weekend and runs on Saturdays until Thanksgiving, from 8 a.m. to 12:30 p.m.

Tourism Red Deer Visitor Centre and Alberta Sports Hall of Fame and Museum

Location: North of the 32nd Street overpass on Hwy 2, Red Deer.
Info: Visitor Centre Hours: from the Victoria Day weekend to the Labour Day weekend open 9 a.m. to 6 p.m. weekdays and 9 a.m. to 7 p.m. weekends; from the Labour Day weekend to Thanksgiving weekend open daily 9 a.m. to 6 p.m.; the rest of the year open 9 a.m. to 5 p.m. from Monday to Friday; 10 a.m. to 5 p.m. on weekends and holidays. 403-346-0180; info@tourismreddeer.net. Sports Hall of Fame hours: from the Victoria Day weekend to Thanksgiving open daily 9 a.m. to 6 p.m.; from after Thanksgiving to the Victoria Day weekend open daily 10 a.m. to 5 p.m. Admission charged; group rates are available. 403-341-8614; www .albertasportshalloffame.com.

Accessible from the highway, Heritage Ranch, just behind the Tourism Red Deer Visitor Centre has picnic and rest areas, washrooms, a playground, an equestrian centre, and trails. The Alberta Sports Hall of Fame encompasses more than 7,000 square feet and includes a multi-sport Virtual Visual System with hockey, baseball, basketball, football, and soccer, in addition to a baseball pitching area, alpine ski machine, 200-metre wheelchair challenge, and other activities.

Red Deer Museum and Art Gallery and Heritage Square

Location: 4525–47A Avenue, Red Deer.
Info: Open daily 12 p.m. to 5 p.m.; on Wednesdays 12 p.m. to 9 p.m. Closed statutory holidays. Admission by donation. 403-309-8405; www.museum.red-deer.ab.ca; museum@reddeer.ca.

Permanent displays at the Red Deer Museum and Art Gallery portray the history of Red Deer's Aboriginal peoples, immigrants, rural life, and the town's growth into a city. Local, national, and international touring exhibits on art, science, and history are also brought in, with exhibitions changing regularly.

Next to the museum, Heritage Square contains historic buildings, including the Norwegian Laft Hus—a museum and cultural centre that preserves and interprets Norwegian-Canadian culture. You can see a wide variety of traditional Norwegian cooking equipment, books, crafts, and gift items you are unlikely find elsewhere. The old Knox Presbyterian Church steeple, a replica of an 1887 log schoolhouse, and Red Deer's oldest building—the Stevenson-Hall Block, which stood at the corner of Ross Street and Gaetz Avenue in the early 1890s—can also be found here.

Waskasoo Park

Location: Access points include Bower Ponds at 4707 Fountain Drive, and Heritage Ranch at 25 Riverview Park; access the McKenzie Trail Recreation Area from 45th Avenue past Kerry Wood Nature Centre; and the Three Mile Bend (off-leash park) at 76 Street East.
Info: www.waskasoopark.ca.

Called a park of many places, Waskasoo Park offers a variety of things to see and do. The park system follows Piper Creek and the Red Deer River and includes all green areas in Red Deer. Bower Ponds are interconnected ponds used for boating and trout fishing. You will find paddle boat and kayak rentals, as well as a concession and washrooms. You can go ice skating or tobogganing here in winter, and you can access extensive cross-country ski trails.

Cronquist House Multicultural Centre, a restored 1911 Edwardian-style farmhouse, overlooks the ponds. Stop here for lunch or tea and enjoy a look at the ethno-cultural displays.

If travelling with young children, do not expect to walk past the Discovery Canyon water play area without stopping. You can relax at a picnic table or on the beach while young ones cool off. Children of all ages ride inflatable tubes in water that is never deeper than 45 centimetres (18 inches). You can bring your own tube or rent one from the clubhouse.

Walk the McKenzie Trails along the main pond near the picnic shelter and playground area to see dozens of Canada geese raising goslings on the islands. Or visit Kin Kanyon for hiking or bike riding on trails through the creek valley. There's a wading pool and playground here, as well as firewood and washrooms.

Fort Normandeau Historic Site and Interpretive Centre

Location: About 7 km from Red Deer. Follow 32nd Street west about 1 km past the Hwy 2 overpass and follow the signs. From Hwy 2, exit on 32nd Street westbound. **Info:** Open 12 p.m. to 5 p.m. from Victoria Day to late June; 12 p.m. to 8 p.m. from June 30 to Labour Day. Wheelchair accessible. 403-347-7550; www.waskasoopark.ca.

Located in Waskasoo Park, the Fort Normandeau Historic Site and Interpretive Centre are at the Red Deer River Crossing, where early travellers once made their way across the water. The crossing was originally part of an Aboriginal trail that ran north from Montana, and across the Bow and Red Deer rivers to Fort Edmonton. When the North West Mounted Police established Fort Calgary in 1875, traffic to Edmonton increased, and the route became known as the Calgary and Edmonton Trail.

In 1884, Robert McClellan built a stopping house for travellers. During the Riel Rebellion, Lt. J. E. Bédard Normandeau, an officer with the 65th Mount Royal Rifles, fortified the stopping house. You can see a replica of the 1885 fort, which was built using some of the original logs. The interpretive centre offers military skirmish re-enactments with costumed soldiers and rebels using black powder weapons.

You will also find a garden, a poultry yard, tipis, a treed picnic area, and a place to launch a canoe or kayak. Those exploring the Waskasoo Park system often start an afternoon paddle here. Every May, on the weekend following Victoria Day, Fort Normandeau Days provide an entire weekend of historic entertainment, with military skirmishes, period foods, children's games, and traditional Aboriginal ceremonies and dancing.

Kerry Wood Nature Centre and Gaetz Lakes Sanctuary

Location: 1.5 km north of 55th Street on 45th Avenue in Red Deer, on the southeast bank of the Red Deer River.

Info: Gaetz Lakes Sanctuary is always open. No pets, cycling, running, in-line skating, cross-country skiing, or motorized vehicles are permitted in the sanctuary. Donations are appreciated, with $2 per person or $5 per family suggested. Kerry Wood Nature Centre hours: from the Victoria Day to the Labour Day weekend open daily 10 a.m. to 8 p.m.; the rest of the year open daily 10 a.m. to 5 p.m.; open 1 p.m. to 5 p.m. on statutory holidays. 403-346-2010; www.waskasoopark.ca.

The Kerry Wood Nature Centre and Gaetz Lakes Sanctuary are an outdoor lover's dream. Named for the late E. A. Kerry Wood—a naturalist, award-winning author, and long-time Red Deer resident—the centre offers nature walks, exhibits, and a unique gift shop that will particularly appeal to birders. The Gaetz Lakes Sanctuary became a protected federal migratory bird sanctuary in 1924. You will find 5 kilometres of trails, a bird blind, and viewing decks. Fed by springs, two oxbow lakes in the reserve attract nesting grebes, coots, and ducks. The many wildflowers include some rare orchids.

Sunnybrook Farm Museum and Interpretive Centre

Location: 4701–30th Street, Red Deer.
Info: Open September through May, Monday to Friday, 10 a.m. to 4 p.m.; daily from June through August, 10 a.m. to 4 p.m. Donations appreciated, and tax receipts are available for amounts greater than $10. 403-340-3511; www.sunnybrookfarm museum.ca.

The 4-hectare (10-acre) Sunnybrook Farm Museum preserves and interprets the history of mixed farming in central Alberta. Originally settled in 1899 by James Bower and family, the farm raised pure-bred cattle and Percheron horses. You can see the barns and workshops built by the Bowers and a century-old pioneer log house moved here from the Evarts district. The museum includes Hudkins and Van Slyke plows, which were both invented in the area, as well as early tractors, binders, rakes, threshing machines, and dairy and blacksmith equipment.

ASPEN BEACH PROVINCIAL PARK (GULL LAKE)

Directions: Exit Edmonton on Hwy 2 south; take exit 422B to Hwy 12 west toward Bentley.
Distance: 144 km, or about 1 hour and 38 minutes, south of Edmonton.
Info: The park may be closed for several weeks in spring due to poor road conditions. 1-877-277-3645.

One of Alberta's first provincial parks, Aspen Beach has wide sand beaches and warm shallow water that attract paddlers, sunbathers, and swimmers. There is a boat launch suitable for small vessels, and opportunities to fish, hike, powerboat, swim, windsurf, and water-ski. Winter activities include ice fishing, as well as cross-country skiing on 4 kilometres of non-groomed trails. The day-use area at Ebeling Beach has change rooms, firepits, flush toilets, and firewood for sale.

PONOKA

Directions: From Edmonton, continue on Hwy 2 south, take exit 450A to access Hwy 53 east toward Ponoka; merge onto Hwy 53, and turn left at Hwy 2A at the crossroads of Hwys 2A and 53.
Distance: 106 km, or about 1 hour and 16 minutes, from Edmonton; about 40 km north from Red Deer.
Info: 403-783-0129; www.ponoka.org.

Originally a railway stop known as Siding 14, *Ponoka* is the Blackfoot word for "elk" or "red deer." Many settlers came to the Battle River valley from eastern Canada and the American Midwest. In 1912, Alberta's first mental health care facility was founded here.

Today more than 6,500 residents live in Ponoka. A downtown stroll reveals well-preserved storefronts in a refurbished town centre. Just south of town, the J. J. Collett Natural Area offers 257 hectares (635 acres) of rolling landscape with trails ideal for orienteering, hiking, and nature observation. Along with western Canada's largest single-day livestock auction, the town hosts a stampede, classic car show and shine, and country fair.

Fort Ostell Museum

Location: 5320–54th Street (at the north end of Centennial Park), Ponoka.
Info: Open from the Victoria Day weekend until the Labour Day weekend, 10 a.m. to 5 p.m. from Tuesday to Friday, and 1 p.m. to 5 p.m. on Sundays and holiday Mondays. From February through May, tours are available upon request from 1 p.m. to 4 p.m. Admission charged. www.fortostellmuseum.com.

The Fort Ostell Museum is named for the 1885 fort built near Ponoka. During the Riel Rebellion, Cree raided the mission and plundered the Hudson Bay store. Under Captain John Benjamin Ostell's leadership, 462 men from Calgary came to build a fortification near the Battle River. The museum has a model of the fort and the original flag that flew here, as well as more than 1,000 pioneer artifacts and memorabilia. Adjacent to the museum, Centennial Park is home to the world's largest bucking horse and also features minigolf.

LACOMBE

Directions: Exit Edmonton on Hwy 2 south, take the off-ramp to Hwy 12 east; or travel Hwy 2 south, take exit 431 for Hwy 2A south, stay left at the fork, and follow signs for Canadian University College/C & E Trail (south), follow Hwy 2A south, and turn right at Hwy 12/50th Avenue.
Distance: 127 km, or about 1 hour and 30 minutes, from Edmonton.
Info: www.lacombe.ca or www.lacombetourism.com.

Surveyed in 1884, the worn path used by wagons and Red River carts on the Calgary and Edmonton Trail (C & E Trail) was the Lacombe area's first transportation route. The original C & E Trail weaves through Lacombe—from the town's southern boundary with the Agricultural

Research Station, and through residential neighbourhoods, ponds, and multi-purpose trails, to its north junction with Highway 2A.

Ed Barnett, Lacombe's first pioneer, settled here in 1883, providing the area's first stopping house. When the railway came, Siding 12 was unofficially called Barnett's Siding, but railway officials chose to name it Lacombe in honour of missionary Father Albert Lacombe—the Blackrobe Voyageur.

Declared a village in 1896, Lacombe incorporated as a town in 1902 and had 900 residents by 1905. The Dominion Government established the Agricultural Research Centre here in 1907, strengthening the town's role as a commercial area; Red Deer, however, grew more quickly and beat out Lacombe as the major centre of the region Lacombe's early growth can still be seen on the most-intact Edwardian main street in Alberta, where many 1900–1930 buildings make the downtown unique and especially picturesque. You can take a walking historical tour to see preserved early-20th-century homes, heritage commercial buildings, and 20 1890–1910 themed murals. Self-guiding maps are available at the Michener House Museum, the Flatiron Interpretive Centre, and several local businesses.

The Lacombe Interpretive Centre (5005–50th Avenue, also called Barnett Avenue) is in the Flatiron Building, named for its resemblance to the profile of a flat iron when viewed from above. It is one of only 13 such buildings in North America. Restored to its original 1900 state, the building contains visitor information, displays, local artifacts, and a theatre showing a film about Lacombe's history.

It is a short walk from here to the Michener House Museum and Archives (5036–51st (Alberta) Street), the 100-year-old birthplace of the Right Honourable Roland Michener, Governor General of Canada from 1967 to 1974. The museum displays period artifacts and hosts various summer events, including a pancake breakfast with the Antique Auto Club. The Lacombe and District Historical Society offers summer walking tours of historic downtown Lacombe. Tours take 30 to 45 minutes and start at Michener House Museum. Groups are preferred. You can buy a self-guided Walking Tour booklet for

$2. The museum is open from Victoria Day through Labour Day, Tuesday to Saturday, from 9 a.m. to 5 p.m. Admission by donation. (403-782-3933.)

One block east, you will find the carefully preserved Blacksmith Shop Museum (5020–49th (Glass) Street). Built in 1902, Lacombe's blacksmith shop is one of only two Alberta blacksmith shops to remain in the locations where they were first built. The museum contains blacksmithing artifacts and a working shop. Call the museum ahead of time if you would like to book a tour or a hand-forging demonstration. If you include a blacksmith shop tour after a historic downtown tour, allow an additional 30 minutes. The museum is open from Victoria Day through Labour Day, Tuesday to Saturday, from 9 a.m. to 5 p.m. Admission by donation. 403-782-9344 or 403-782-7333.

Today, almost 12,000 people live in Lacombe. The numbered downtown streets also have signs with Lacombe's old street names, which were added as a centennial project. Annual events include the Vintage Machinery Club Show, Lacombe Days, and Lacombe Art Exhibit and Sale.

Ellis Bird Farm

Location: 16 km from Lacombe. Exit Lacombe south on Hwy 2 or 2A, turn east onto Hwy 597, then north onto Prentiss Road (Range Road 26-0); alternatively, exit Red Deer on Hwy 11, turn north onto Freedom Road, then west on Hwy 597 and north on Prentiss Road (Range Road 26-0).
Info: Open from the Victoria Day weekend to Labour Day weekend, Tuesday to Sunday and holiday Mondays, 11 a.m. to 5 p.m. 403-885-4477 or 403-346-2211. Extensive wheelchair path available.

A working farm, the Ellis Bird Farm is dedicated to conserving mountain bluebirds, tree swallows, and other nesting birds native to central Alberta. Visitors can meander along trails, through hummingbird, butterfly, wildflower, and water gardens, and see the world's largest outdoor bluebird nest box collection. There is a visitor centre and tea house.

The Lacombe Corn Maze

Location: 5 km west of Lacombe. From Hwy 2 south, take the off-ramp to Hwy 12 west; turn south onto Range Road 27-3.
Info: Open from the last weekend in July to the Saturday following Thanksgiving. Closed Sundays. 403-302-1709; www.lacombecornmaze.com.

The Lacombe Corn Maze boasts a 6-hectare (15-acre) maze of corn 3 metres tall or higher. Attractions include a corn cannon, cow train, mini mazes, hay jump, farm animals, a unique goat walk, and picnic sites with firepits. Be sure to wear sturdy shoes when planning to trek through a corn maze.

INNISFAIL

Directions: Exit Edmonton on Hwy 2 south, take Exit 368 to access Hwy 54 west toward Caroline/Innisfail; merge onto Hwy 590.
Distance: 183 km, or about 1 hour and 50 minutes, from Edmonton.
Info: 403-227-3376; www.townofinnisfail.com/tourism.htm.

Innisfail was once a stopping place for stagecoaches and travellers on the Calgary and Edmonton Trail. Before the Canadian Pacific Railway gave Innisfail its Celtic name, which means Isle of Destiny, the community was known as Poplar Grove. In 1754, Anthony Henday travelled here on a Hudson Bay Company fur-trading mission, accompanied by members of the Cree tribe. From a hill just east of Innisfail, Henday became the first European to see the Canadian Rockies. Today, almost 8,000 people live here.

RCMP Police Dog Service Training Centre

Location: Just south of Innisfail. Travel south on Hwy 2, take Exit 365 east, and follow the signs.
Info: Demonstrations are held every Wednesday at 2 p.m. for 45 to 60 minutes, from about the third weekend in May to mid-September. Large groups must book in advance. 403-227-3346; policedogs@rcmp-grc.gc.ca.

The RCMP Police Dog Service Training Centre trains dogs and handlers, and provides police dogs to agencies across Canada. The centre welcomes visitors to its facilities and offers free public demonstrations during the summer.

Innisfail and District Historical Village

Location: 42nd Street and 52nd Avenue, Innisfail.
Info: Open from mid-May to early September, Wednesday to Sunday, 11 a.m. to 5:30 p.m. Donations accepted. 403-227-2906 (summer), 403-227-3847, or 403-227-3405; www.innisfailhistory.com; idhs@incentre.net.

The Innisfail and District Historical Village includes 17 pioneer buildings and a farm machinery collection. You can see the only stopping house preserved from the days of stagecoach travel between Calgary and Edmonton. Each building is furnished to interpret area history up to the 1940s. Tea is held every Friday in the Tea Room from 2 p.m. to 4 p.m., from the first Friday in June through the first Friday in September. Special summer activities include Canada Day celebrations, Fiddlers' Jamboree & Strawberry Festival, Harvest Festival, and Oktoberfest.

Stephansson House Provincial Historic Site

Location: 22 km northwest of Innisfail. Exit Innisfail on Hwy 2 north, take the Penhold turnoff and follow Hwy 42 west through Penhold; continue west on Hwy 592, follow the signs and turn right (north) at the Markerville turnoff, and follow signs to site.
Info: Open daily May 15 to Labour Day, 10 a.m. to 6 p.m. Admission charged. 403-728-3929 in summer, 780-427-1787 year-round; www.culture.alberta.ca/sh/.

Born in Iceland in 1853, Stephan G. Stephansson brought his family to the Markerville area in 1889. Stephansson is considered one of the greatest poets in the Western world, and in Iceland his work is studied for its linguistic and poetic merit. A pioneer, Stephansson laboured in the fields by day, composing poems in his head as he worked—sometimes dashing inside to write down a few lines. No other Canadian poet has created as much as this prolific writer, who published more than 2,000 pages of poetry.

A provincial historic site, Stephansson's home was restored to its original appearance in 1927—the year Stephansson died. Costumed guides provide interpretive programs and tours. You can see how wool was spun and how other household chores were managed, or enjoy a poetry reading—1920s style.

SYLVAN LAKE

Directions: Exit Edmonton on Hwy 2 south, and take exit 405B to Hwy 11A west toward Sylvan Lake.
Distance: 163 km, or about 1 hour and 50 minutes, from Edmonton.
Info: www.town.sylvan.lake.ab.ca.

Known by a number of names, including Snake Lake and Swan Lake, Sylvan Lake's final name comes from the Latin word *sylvanus,* meaning "of a forest." The first settlers came in 1899, and by 1904 the lakeshore already looked like a summer resort—with a hotel, store, post office, and cottages.

In the heart of the Town of Sylvan Lake, the provincial park offers day-use recreation on its 1.6-kilometre beach—one of Alberta's longest stretches of sandy shoreline. More than one million visitors come here every year—perhaps because the town and lake offer something to please all ages, and this includes every water sport imaginable, with boats, Jet Skis, and charters available for rent. You can take a 3-hour paddlewheel tour or experience Wild Rapids Waterslides, western Canada's largest outdoor waterslide park. Non-swimmers will enjoy the many shops and ice-cream opportunities across from the beach.

Sylvan Lake hosts numerous events, including 1913 Days, Dragon Boat Races, Bullz on the Beach, open-water swimming championships, and a Half Ironman Triathlon. Winter visitors missing the beach can check out the popular Polar Dip during the February Winterfest.

RIMBEY

Directions: Exit Edmonton on Hwy 2 south, take exit 450B to Hwy 53 west, then turn left at Hwy 20A.
Distance: 145 km, or about 1 hour and 43 minutes, from Edmonton.
Info: www.rimbey.com.

A town of just more than 2,250 people, Rimbey was named after its first settlers—the Rimbey brothers. Incorporated as a village in 1919 and a town in 1948, Rimbey sits in the scenic Blindman River Valley among the rolling hills that border the Rocky Mountains.

The Early Days Walking Tour encompasses 35 different historic locations that introduce you to town ghosts and historic buildings—with 4 kilometres of walking over a leisurely 2 hours. Pick up a self-guided tour brochure at the town office (4938–50th Avenue).

Pas-Ka-Poo Park, Pioneer Museum, and Smithson International Truck Museum

Location: 51st Avenue and 56th Street, Rimbey.
Info: Open daily 10 a.m. to 5 p.m. Admission charged. 403-843-2004; paskapoo@telus.net.

Pas Ka Poo is Cree for the "Blindman River." The Pas-Ka-Poo Park includes a historical village, 2 museums, and 10 historic buildings, including a 1920s barbershop, railway station, schoolhouse, homestead cottage, and trapper's cabin. Museum collections encompass household items, farm machinery, and the "World's Largest Collection of International Trucks"—with 19 restored International half-ton trucks, including a 1957 International anniversary edition half-ton.

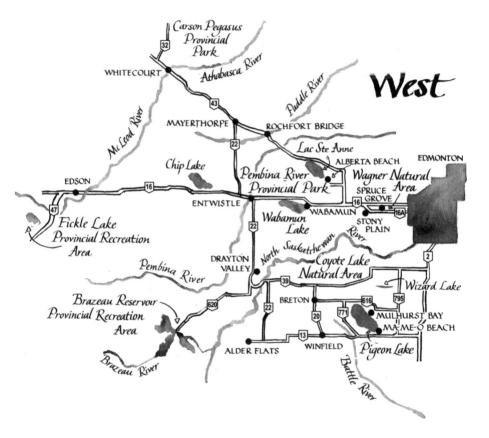

West

WEST OF EDMONTON

Go West! The tendency of Edmontonians to make a beeline for the mountains when heading west is a natural impulse, but an unfortunate one as well. It is common among many residents of major cities: they neglect to enjoy the pleasures near their own backyards in favour of more distant and dramatic landscapes. It is also unnecessary, for in less than 30 minutes, anyone leaving the outskirts of Edmonton's west end can experience an area rich in recreational opportunities for both outdoor enthusiasts and those who want to explore prairie history and culture.

The tri-municipal area of Spruce Grove, Stony Plain, and Parkland County is dotted with rolling hills, pot-hole lakes, beaches, and woodlands. Groves of aspen and spruce alternate with farmers' fields where wheat, oats, barley, canola, and alfalfa thrive in the rich black chernozemic soil. It is not uncommon to see whitetail and mule deer grazing, a coyote loping across a field, or a fox hunting mice in the ditch. Acreage owners sometimes report moose bedding down on their lawns, and hikers on local trails may spot one of these aptly nicknamed swamp donkeys. Porcupines and Richardson's ground squirrels often try to cross highways, overconfident with a seeming sense of immortality. Red-tailed hawks circle above or perch on fence posts, missing none of the activity around them.

The first stop on this day trip through Parkland County will especially appeal to anyone who enjoys natural history. Wagner Bog is a preservation area, set aside for its unique habitat of rare plants, and the presence of birds not seen in other parts of Alberta. Onward to the

SIMPLE SUMMER FAMILY DAY TRIP

Total driving time: about 2 hours and 35 minutes if going to Pembina,
or 2 hours and 15 minutes if choosing Alberta Beach.

Start a pleasant day with your family by heading west to the **Wagner Natural Area** (page 133) to walk the easy 1-hour looping trail through this unique habitat. Return to Hwy 16 and stop in Spruce Grove to tour the **Alberta Honey Producers Co-op** (page 136) on a weekday or **Heritage Grove Park** (page 136), where you'll find a splash area and access to beautiful woodland trails.

When lunchtime comes around, consider visiting the 1950s-style Jack's Drive-In, a local landmark that locals describe as the place to find the best burgers and ice cream made with real cream (123 First Ave, parallel with Hwy 16A).

Continue west to Stony Plain and pull into **Rotary Park and Tourist Information** (page 140), where you will find a train caboose, playground, pond, gazebo, and picnic tables. Your next stop will take you to the **Multicultural Heritage Centre** and **Oppertshauser House** (page 141). You can browse artifacts, as well as visit the general store, and stroll around the award-winning grounds. If you have room for dessert, the Homesteader's Kitchen (Open daily, 11:30 a.m.–4:30 p.m.) is well appreciated for its selection of pies. After your pie, a stroll around town to view the giant murals will feel great!

If you're looking to cool off on a hot day, head to **Pembina River Provincial Park** (page 148) for rock hunting and tubing down the river, or choose to stop off at **Alberta Beach on Lac Ste. Anne** (page 147), for sandcastles and swimming in the warm, shallow water. Plan to have a picnic supper at either of these two locations before heading home.

city of Spruce Grove, you will find more opportunities for hiking, as well as a chance to visit the Bee Maid Honey processing plant. Here you can see first-hand how honey gets from the farm to your table. The next stop takes you to Stony Plain, the town with the painted past. A stroll down Main Street presents larger-than-life murals illustrating the joys and struggles of the early pioneers who first came to the area. Museums bristle with artifacts, while a demonstration farm within town limits provides an up-close experience of agriculture.

Leaving Stony Plain in pursuit of outdoor recreation can take you in many different directions. You may choose lakes for swimming, lakes for boating, or lakes with elaborate trail systems along their shores. With so many recreation areas, it will take more than one day trip to experience all this region has to offer.

Continuing west will take you through to Wabamun Lake, where year-round open water attracts birds and other wildlife. The Pembina River tempts water lovers and fossil hunters, while Lac Ste. Anne draws both the beach crowd and those interested in the annual spiritual pilgrimage that draws thousands to its shores every July. Pigeon Lake also offers a mix of recreation and historical sites, where missionaries and Aboriginal people came together in settlements on the lake's shores.

South and west of Edmonton you can discover the history of North America's largest oil field and how it changed Alberta communities like Drayton Valley. The construction of the railway also had a significant influence on Alberta's first settlements. You will see the tracks necessitated by the "iron horse" in more than one community.

Toward Edson, fields alternating with aspen give way to large stands of lodgepole pine, which increase opportunities to view wildlife and enjoy wilderness settings. Edson is one of the largest towns in Alberta and experiences some of the province's heaviest traffic flow, with about 8,000 vehicles passing through daily.

The drive to Mayerthorpe and Whitecourt gives one the feeling of travelling to communities less influenced by Edmonton's proximity. Both towns are launching points for those interested in excellent

TOWN OF STONY PLAIN

Rotary Park, Stony Plain (page 140)

fishing, boating, water-skiing, swimming, and sailing. You can see an old trapper cabin or learn how the forestry industry operates. Mayerthorpe is the northern link of the 700-kilometre Cowboy Trail, which extends from Cardston to Mayerthorpe. The trail defines the area that first drew both Aboriginal people and European settlers. Rich with Western art, culture, and hospitality, the Cowboy Trail includes three communities in the day-trip zone west of Edmonton.

For more information:
- Drayton Valley & Area
  1-800-633-0899; www.brazeautourism.ca
- Evansburg/Entwistle
  www.partnersonthepembina.com
- Mayerthorpe
  780-786-2416; www.mayerthorpe.ca
- Cowboy Trail Tourism Association
  1-866-627-3051; www.thecowboytrail.com

WAGNER NATURAL AREA

Directions: Follow Hwy 16 west; beyond the Secondary Hwy 794 overpass, turn south onto Atim Road (Range Road 270) and immediately turn left again onto the access road, which leads 150 metres east to a dead-end gravel parking area and the trail entrance.

Distance: 6.5 km from Edmonton city limits.

Info: Admission is free. Year-round access. 780-456-9046. Rubber boots are advised if there has been rain. The use of mosquito repellent will make your hike infinitely more enjoyable. Visitors to natural areas are advised to stay on the trails and refrain from picking plants. http://wagner.fanweb.ca.

Locally known as Wagner Bog, this unique natural area is a jewel on the edge of the city. Its 219 hectares (541 acres) are made up of several habitats not normally found together. The fen is an area rich in minerals and fed by groundwater. You will see marl ponds, black spruce muskeg forest, and willow-sedge fens, as well as upland woods and meadows.

The 1.2-kilometre self-guided hiking trail loops around the startlingly clear water of a fen. The trail continues through wooded areas that are so lush in wet years you can almost imagine you have taken an exotic vacation to a more distant locale. About one-third of all Alberta's plant species can be found at Wagner Bog. It is home to 16 of the province's 26 wild orchid species, and more than 330 other flowering plants. This includes some carnivorous species—fortunately only hungry for insects! There are 138 species of birds, and 800 species of insects, including 35 types of butterflies. Bog visitors may get a close look at western toads and boreal chorus frogs. Wood frogs also live here, and toad walks are held during the spring. Aquatic life is easy to view through the clear water, and children will especially enjoy searching for caddis fly casings and tadpoles.

Birdwatchers should look for least flycatchers, yellow-rumped warblers, dark-eyed juncos, and typical boreal species like the ruby-crowned kinglet and boreal chickadee. Pileated woodpeckers and northern goshawks like the mature forest. Listen for saw-whet and great horned owls at dusk.

SPRUCE GROVE

Directions: Exit Edmonton west on Hwy 16 and continue to Spruce Grove.
Distance: 32.5 km west of Edmonton.
Info: 780-962-2611; www.sprucegrove.org.

Both poplar and spruce trees are prominent in the Spruce Grove area west of Edmonton. The community's founders debated naming the community Poplar Grove but then discovered that a place with this name already existed.

French and Scottish pioneers came in 1891, setting up a general store, blacksmith shop, hotel, Roman Catholic Church, and livery

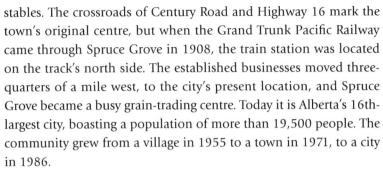

stables. The crossroads of Century Road and Highway 16 mark the town's original centre, but when the Grand Trunk Pacific Railway came through Spruce Grove in 1908, the train station was located on the track's north side. The established businesses moved three-quarters of a mile west, to the city's present location, and Spruce Grove became a busy grain-trading centre. Today it is Alberta's 16th-largest city, boasting a population of more than 19,500 people. The community grew from a village in 1955 to a town in 1971, to a city in 1986.

As you enter Spruce Grove along Highway 16A, watch for the 1958 grain elevator that holds the Spruce Grove Grain Elevator Museum and Saturday farmers' market. (100 Railway Avenue; open from late April to mid-December 9:30 a.m. to 2:30 p.m. 780-962-0830.) And stop in to tour one of Canada's oldest working grain elevators, which is open from June through September, Tuesday through Saturday, 9 a.m. to 3 p.m. (780-960-4600.) You can visit the archive Tuesday mornings from 10 a.m. to 12 p.m.

Spruce Grove's Horizon Stage is one of those lovely theatres large enough to bring in spectacular entertainment but small enough for every seat to be a good one. The theatre seats more than 300 people and offers all kinds of live entertainment including music, theatre, comedy, and performances for family audiences. (780-962-8995; www.horizonstage.com.)

The Melcor Cultural Centre (35–5th Avenue, in King Street Mall) is home to the Allied Arts Council–Spruce Grove Art Gallery, which features works by Canadian artists in watercolour, pastel, acrylic, clay, wood, and a variety of other artistic mediums. The gallery is open 10 a.m. to 8 p.m. from Monday through Thursday, and 10 a.m. to 5 p.m. on Friday and Saturday. Admission is free. (780-962-0664; www.allied artscouncil.com.)

Annual events include the Canada Day and Street Performers Festival, Grove Cruise–Classic Car Weekend, Halloween Hoopla, and Christmas in Central Park.

Heritage Grove Park

Location: From Hwy 16 westbound, take the Century Road exit south. Turn west on Grove Drive, then south on King Street. Watch for the Log Cabin Interpretive Centre and Park Staging Area on the east side of the road.

The mature trees that give the city of Spruce Grove its name can be seen in abundance at Heritage Grove Park. This 50-hectare area features picnic grounds, 15 kilometres of trails, and outdoor interpretive displays depicting the area's geology, geography, vegetation, history, birds, and wildlife. The trails allow easy walking through natural woodlands and are ideal for jogging, cycling, or in-line skating. Young summertime visitors will enjoy the splash park. Winter attractions include a skating oval and the Hamburger Hill toboggan run, as well as opportunities for cross-country skiing.

Alberta Honey Producers Co-op

Location: 70 Alberta Avenue, Spruce Grove. From Hwy 16A, turn south on Golden Spike Road, and turn west at the first turn onto Alberta Avenue.
Info: Open from March to October, Monday to Friday, 8 a.m. to 5 p.m.; from November 1 until the end of February, Monday to Friday, 8 a.m. to 4:30 p.m. 780-962-5573; www.beemaid.com.

Called the Honey Processing Capital of Canada, Spruce Grove is home to the Alberta Honey Producers Co-op, where Bee Maid products are produced from the clover-flavoured honey collected by western prairie beekeepers. A tour through the Bee Maid plant will leave you longing to dip your finger into a bowl of sweet, sticky honey. Fortunately, a trip through the gift shop offers the opportunity to satisfy this desire. The store also contains items of interest to cooks and those who make candles. There is no charge for tours; however, there is a nominal fee if you want to roll your own beeswax candle. Individuals interested in tours should call ahead to make sure a guide is available. Group tours can also be pre-arranged throughout the year, except during a two-week shutdown period in July.

STONY PLAIN

Directions: Exit Edmonton from either Hwy 16 or 16A west, and take the Stony Plain exit onto Secondary Hwy 779 (Range Road 10), which becomes 48th Street.
Distance: 20 km west of Edmonton.
Info: 780-963-2151; www.stonyplain.com.

In the early 1700s a small band of Stoney from the Dakotas came to the foothills east of the Rocky Mountains, between the Bow and Athabasca rivers. Because of the Stoney Indians and the fertile plains where they camped, the region west of Fort Edmonton became known as the Stoney plains.

John L. McDonald moved to the area more than 100 years ago and built a house near a creek flowing from Dog Lake. A bend in the creek looked like the rear end of a dog, and hence the Cree called it *Atim Ozwe Sipi*—meaning "dog creek" or "dog rump creek."

The area around the town came to be known as Stoney, but the town was called Dog Rump Creek. The community changed its name to Stony Plain in 1892 after J. L. McDonald applied to open a post office. He dropped the "e" from "Stoney" in the hope that it would stop people from thinking the area was covered in stones. However, in 1858, James Hector of the Palliser Expedition noted the town deserved its name, for the plain was covered with boulders, which are generally rare in this region.

In 1906 the railway from Edmonton passed more than 1.5 kilometres from Stony Plain, and community leaders decided to move the town closer to the tracks. They rolled the buildings on logs to the spot where the town is today—a task that required 20 teams of horses.

Stony Plain became a tent city of railway workers; indeed, its first bank opened in a tent. In 1907 Israel Umbach was sworn in as sheriff, and a year later Stony Plain became a town. Umbach is remembered for chaining himself to a locomotive on the railway tracks to force the CPR to pay its outstanding taxes.

Stony Plain is an agricultural community with a population that has grown to more than 12,000 people. You can experience much of Stony Plain's charm by strolling the historic downtown, which is adorned with a heritage theme comprising old-fashioned lamp posts and park benches, as well as colourful flowering baskets in the summer. Dubbed the Town with the Painted Past, Stony Plain has been called the wall-art capital of Alberta, the result of its Outdoor Gallery that appears on the outside walls of many buildings and increases in size annually. So far, 26 larger-than-life murals and a sculpture showcase the community's history. Both local and nationally known artists have illustrated Stony Plain's colourful past with artwork that depicts the town's multiculturalism, early pioneers, and landmarks. You can pick up a brochure to guide you through the town's Outdoor Gallery at the tourist information centre and many main-street shops. The Multicultural Heritage Centre arranges a variety of guided tours.

You will find abundant green spaces, including the ornamental garden Shikaoi Park, named after Stony Plain's sister community in Hokkaido, Japan. The "Many Faces, One Heart" mural at the park pays tribute to the town's multiculturalism. More than 14 kilometres of trails, with wooden bridges, crisscross the beautiful Whispering Waters Creek that flows through town. Trails lead to a public BMX bike track, skateboard park, picnic area with cookstoves and firewood, as well as two gazebos.

If you enjoy home-baked, handcrafted, and home-grown goods, visit the Stony Plain Country Market. Local vendors sell their goods at the Stony Plain Exhibition Grounds (5120–43rd Avenue) from late May to mid-October on Saturdays from 9 a.m. to 1 p.m. From November through April, these goods are sold on the second Saturday of the month at the PERC (Parkland Educational Resource Centre) building (5413–51st Street), from 1 p.m. to 4 p.m. A farmers' market is also held on Saturdays from April through December at the downtown Stony Plain Community Centre (5008–51st Avenue), from 9 a.m. to 1 p.m.

Annual events include Farmers' Days and Kinsmen Rodeo, Canada Day festivities, Great White North Triathlon, Blueberry Bluegrass and

Stony Plain Tourist Information

TOWN OF STONY PLAIN

Rotary Park, Stony Plain

Country Festival, Cowboy Poetry and Country Music Gathering, and Pioneer Harvest Old Time Thrashing Bee.

Rotary Park and Tourist Information

Location: 4815–44th Avenue, Stony Plain. Enter the town along Secondary Hwy 779 (Range Road 10), which becomes 48th Street, and watch for the park's double pond on the west side of the road. Turn west on 44th Avenue to access the park's entrance.
Info: Tourist information hours: Monday to Friday, 8:30 a.m. to 4:30 p.m.; extended hours in July and August: weekdays, 8 a.m. to 6 p.m., and weekends and holidays, 9:30 a.m. to 5:30 p.m. 780-963-4545.

Also called Dog Rump Creek, Rotary Park is a good choice for your first Stony Plain stop. The chamber of commerce offers year-round visitor information inside a replica of the Stony Plain Canadian Northern Railway Station built in 1905. You can see an assortment of train equipment, including a restored railway car. Children will also appreciate the playground and a jaunt across the wooden bridge. Near the fountain in the pond, the gazebo provides welcome shade on hot summer days and is a pleasant place to enjoy a snack. In winter, the double pond is cleared and flooded for ice-skating. A skate change room is available.

Multicultural Heritage Centre

Location: 5411–51st Street, Stony Plain.
Info: Museum and store are open daily, 10 a.m. to 4 p.m.; Homesteader's Kitchen is open daily 11:30 a.m. to 3 p.m. for meals, and until 4 p.m. for pie and beverages. Donations accepted. 780-963-2777; www.multicentre.org.

The Multicultural Heritage Centre is housed in a 1925 building that once held the first regional high school west of Edmonton. White lettering above the entrance reminds visitors of its origin as the Old Brick School. Now a provincial historic site, about 85,000 people visit the renovated centre every year. The grounds outside are as charming as the building's interior.

One room in the centre portrays the lives of European pioneers who came to the area in the 1890s. This living museum, known as the Settler's Cabin, contains more than 3,600 artifacts. The smell of the wood-burning stove and taste of hand-cranked ice cream make the experience even more authentic, as do the fresh pies and bread, made on-site every morning in the Homesteader's Kitchen restaurant.

In addition to historical displays and exhibits, the Multicultural Heritage Centre contains the Wild Rose Historical Library and Archives and the Multicultural Heritage Centre Public Art Gallery. The museum hosts several activities throughout the year, and summertime visits are made especially pleasant given the opportunity to dine outdoors near flowerbeds, fountains, and goldfish ponds.

Look for Oppertshauser House next to the Multicultural Heritage Centre. The Oppertshauser family opened a store in Stony Plain in 1901, and today their 1910 house is used to display furnishings from the 1920s, '30s, and '40s. You can touch many of the artifacts on display, making a visit here very satisfying if you enjoy a hands-on experience. Be sure to note the late-1800s organ, and peer through the house's original glass windows.

In honour of its namesake, Oppertshauser House is home to a general store. The shop sells museum-quality reproductions of items available in the 1920s, '30s, and '40s, including children's toys, ink-wells, and slates.

Immediately south of the Multicultural Heritage Centre and Oppertshauser House, a 2-hectare (5-acre) farm is used to demonstrate contemporary agricultural practices; the farm grows fresh food for the Multicultural Heritage Centre restaurant and Stony Plain Country Market. Signs identify crop names and more than 300 planted trees. You will find a stream, waterfall, and pond on the property, as well as an old homestead that was moved here for development in the future. The community garden contains at least 55 different types of vegetables on more than 720 square metres.

Stony Plain and District Pioneer Museum

Location: 5120–43rd Avenue, Stony Plain. Enter through the South Exhibition Park gates, and drive to the south end of the park.
Info: Open April 1 to October 31. Museum hours: from Monday to Saturday, 10 a.m. to 4 p.m., on Sundays 1 p.m. to 4 p.m. Tea house hours: Friday and Saturday, 11 a.m. to 4 p.m. New facilities will open in the winter of 2009, with a possible change in hours. Donations accepted. 780-963-1234.

The Stony Plain and District Pioneer Museum is housed in seven buildings stocked with more than 5,000 items donated by area residents. The museum includes a natural history corner with an antler collection, animal skulls, and mounted birds. You will see numerous items that depict early pioneer lifestyles, including farm tools, household items, and wood stoves. Items of particular interest include pump organs, telephone switchboards from the 1920s, and a bucket made out of paper in the late 1800s.

A collection of battered luggage hints at the hardships of pioneer travel. One suitcase is almost 200 years old. Russian, German, and

Stony Plain and District Pioneer Museum

Austrian immigrants carried these suitcases as they left their home-lands—some to escape war, others to leave growing populations and crowded conditions, and still others to seek better opportunities.

You can also see a 1909 schoolhouse that was converted to a church, a 1914 house, an 1892 farmhouse replica, and a 1922 log cabin converted to a tea house. There are dozens of old farm machines, a 1923 fire-fighting wagon that was pulled by horses, and buggies from the late 1920s and early 1930s. Each carriage, tractor, thresher, wagon, and set of racks is in working condition. Every fall, a threshing bee is held to demonstrate an old-time harvest. A 1928 tractor is used to pull a 1928 threshing machine, and teams of horses are hitched to racks to bring in the crop.

Hasse Lake

Location: 14.4 km from Stony Plain. Exit Stony Plain on Secondary Hwy 628 west.
Info: Horses and motorized vehicles are not allowed on trails.

This 121-hectare (300-acre) day-use area set in an aspen forest is an ideal family destination. The terrain around the sandy beach forms natural barriers that are handy for parents who need to keep young children in sight. A playground on the beach, picnic tables, firepits, boat launch, and pier make this a pleasant place to enjoy a picnic. Trout fishing is popular here, and boaters with small craft are welcome, providing they travel slower than 12 kilometres per hour. A small island in the lake is typically covered in birds, including pelicans, gulls, sandpipers, and other shorebirds.

When hiking the easy 3-kilometre loop, note the elaborate beaver runs and watch for wildflowers such as Western Canada violet, wild lily of the valley, fairybells, and sarsaparilla. Children catching minnows may net a threespine stickleback, a fish illegally introduced into Hasse Lake in the late 1970s.

The park is a pleasant place to visit in the winter. Ice fishing is popular, and the 3-kilometre trail is groomed for cross-country skiing.

Chickakoo Lake Recreation Area

Location: 13 km from Stony Plain. Exit Stony Plain on Secondary Hwy 779; turn left (west) at Township Road 534. Drive 5 km (3 miles), then turn right (north) onto Range Road 12A and continue on to Range Road 13. Directional signs along the route will guide you.

Chickakoo Lake Recreation Area is a 194-hectare (480 acre) park located on the ancient delta of a glacier. It encompasses seven small lakes and two ponds. Maps at the park entrance detail more than 14 kilometres of trails that include easy walks and more challenging hikes. A self-guided interpretive tour along one of the trails details park flora and fauna.

Mountain bikers, horseback riders, and hikers will find exploring these hills and valleys a pleasurable experience. Bring your binoculars and camera because wildlife is plentiful. This is also a good place to paddle a canoe or fish for brook trout.

Once enough snow falls, trails are groomed for all levels of cross-country skiing. A chalet is available from November through April.

WABAMUN LAKE PROVINCIAL PARK

Directions: Exit Edmonton on either Hwy 16 or 16A west, take the Hwy 30 (Range Road 35) exit, and turn left onto Hwy 30 south.
Distance: 67 km, or about 50 minutes, from Edmonton.
Info: 780-892-2702.

Wabamun Lake was originally known as White Whale Lake because of its large whitefish. In 1906 the name was changed to Wabamun, which is Cree for "looking glass." Established in 1955, Wabamun Lake Provincial Park is a choice destination for people interested in picnicking, hiking, swimming, snorkelling, scuba diving, sailing, boating, water-skiing, windsurfing, and fishing.

In the park's day-use area, the beach is near picnic sites and horseshoe pits, as well as a baseball diamond and soccer field. Two boat launches are available, including a paved ramp for trailers and a hand-launch site for Jet Skis and sailboards. From the beach, you can hike along Moonlight Bay, where interpretive signs identify park plants and animals.

In 1868, Moonlight Bay was the site of the White Whale Stopping House, where as many as 30 tired travellers could spend the night and shelter their horses. The upstairs sleeping area was a large room with many bunks and no privacy. The stopping house closed in about 1912 when the railway changed how people travelled.

Today, visitors to Wabamun Lake are likely to notice the Sundance power plant located across the lake. Coal is abundant in the Wabamun area, and the Sundance plant is western Canada's largest coal-fired electrical generating facility. Interpretive signs in the park explain how electricity is produced and address environmental concerns. The Sundance plant's thermal output makes Wabamun the only Alberta lake where you can fish in open water throughout the year. Boaters can use the lake for about two extra months each year.

Wintertime at Wabamun means the chance to enjoy a lit ice-skating area, as well as 6 kilometres of beginner-level ski trails along Moonlight Bay. A heated shelter is located at the trailhead.

SEBA BEACH MUSEUM AND HERITAGE WALL

Directions: Exit Edmonton on either Hwy 16 or 16A west, and head south on Hwy 759 (Range Road 60) to reach Seba Beach. The museum is on Main Avenue and 101 Street North.
Distance: 89 km, or about 1 hour and 5 minutes, from Edmonton.
Info: In June, open on the weekends; from July 1 through to Labour Day, open from Wednesday to Sunday as well as holidays. Hours are 10 a.m. to 5 p.m. Admission is free, but donations are appreciated. 780-797-3863.

Located on Wabamun Lake's west end, Seba Beach has been a lakeside retreat since 1906, when the first homesteaders—R. P. (Perly) Cull and Arthur Hovey—arrived from Quebec. Looking for an area with good fishing and hunting, they chose the west side of Wabamun Lake. You can see their original cabin, called Massawippi Cottage, at the corner of 5th Street South and 1st Avenue.

The Seba Beach Museum and Heritage Wall is a charming and well-laid-out museum that includes a fascinating collection of pioneer artifacts, such as a boat motor, early ice skates, regatta trophies, and photographs. You will find the 1946 All Saints Anglican Church and the original Seba Beach village office, as well as Seba Beach history depicted on the Heritage Wall. A museum pamphlet includes a list of historical sites you can walk to, including the 1916 YWCA hostel, the Silver Dollar Dance Hall, and Chummy's Store and Dance Hall, built before 1924.

Local amenities and attractions in the Summer Village of Seba Beach include a general store, restaurant, and minigolf. A weekly farmers' market is held from 11 a.m. to 12:30 p.m. on Saturdays, from

May to the end of August, at the Pavilion Bingo Hall on Main Street. The Seba Beach Regatta is held on the August long weekend.

ALBERTA BEACH ON LAC STE. ANNE

Directions: Exit Edmonton on Hwy 16 or 16A west, turn north onto Hwy 43, then turn west onto Secondary Hwy 633.
Distance: 60 km west, or about 45 minutes, of Edmonton.
Info: 780-924-3181; www.albertabeach.com.

The Cree knew Lac Ste. Anne as *Manito Sakahigan*, meaning "Spirit Lake." White traders later called it Devil's Lake because storms could quickly cause the lake to become dangerous. In August 1843, Father Thibault named it Lac Sainte Anne, and it became the site of the first permanent Catholic mission west of Winnipeg.

Lac Ste. Anne is home to a famous Catholic pilgrimage. Thousands of people converge here every summer to celebrate their spirituality and seek healing in the sacred water of Lac Ste. Anne. The pilgrimage has occurred since 1889 and coincides with the July 26 feast day of Sainte Anne. Masses are given in Cree, Chipewyan, Blackfoot, Dene, and English. Once, as many as 30,000 people participated.

On the southeast side of the lake, the village of Alberta Beach is home to more than 750 permanent residents, but the population expands on summer weekends—sometimes to more than 3,000 people. Originally developed as a railway community, Alberta Beach was incorporated as a summer village in 1925.

People come to Alberta Beach for swimming, windsurfing, water-skiing, sailing, fishing, jet skiing, and boating. The village has a resort feel to it, with stores, restaurants, and pubs all within walking distance of the beach. Lac Ste. Anne is the kind of lake where you can walk a long way out and the warm water will only be up to your knees. The sandy shore has a roped swimming area, playground, and long pier. You can rent a variety of watercraft just off the main beach.

Or, if you visit in winter, come for ice fishing, snowmobiling, ice skating, or cross-country skiing.

PEMBINA RIVER PROVINCIAL PARK

Directions: Exit Edmonton on Hwy 16 west; take the Hwy 22 (Range Road 74) exit toward Entwistle. At the fork, stay right and follow the signs for Hwy 16A west to access Pembina River Provincial Park.
Distance: 106 km, or about 1 hour and 15 minutes, from Edmonton.
Info: Before entering the river, ensure your safety by asking park staff about the river's current conditions. Identify where you will get off the river before you start, because it is not marked. 780-727-3643.

Pembina River Provincial Park is located near the towering Pembina River gorge, where cliffs rise up to 62 metres from the rocky riverbed. Retreating glacial meltwater created the gorge during the Wisconsin Age, between 75,000 and 10,000 years ago.

Visitors ride inner tubes and air mattresses down the river, which winds around the campground. Depending on water levels, this refreshing trip takes about an hour to complete. Put in at the beach near the park gate and exit at the trail adjacent to the amphitheatre. The walk back to the starting point takes about 15 to 20 minutes.

The park has an interpretive trail and viewpoint; there are opportunities to swim, canoe, kayak, fish, hike, and play horseshoes and volleyball. Amenities include a playground, cook shelter, firepits, and both flush and pit toilets.

In 1862 gold seekers paddled the Pembina River near modern-day Entwistle on their way to the tempting Cariboo goldfields. A farming community, Entwistle is home to 460 people, but in 1909 it was much busier, with as many as 3,000 homesteaders living within a 48-kilometre radius. Rails were laid from Stony Plain to Entwistle in the fall of 1909, but stopped at the daunting Pembina River gorge. As the end of the line, Entwistle thrived as businesses provided goods and services to settlers moving farther west; the town also catered to the several hundred men working on the Grand Trunk Pacific Railroad trestle.

Entwistle was called the toughest town in the Canadian northwestern frontier. Moonshine was freely sold, and four houses of ill repute, in addition to gambling joints, were in operation until the 1909 arrival of five Royal North West Mounted Police. When the Pembina River bridge was completed in 1910, construction gangs moved west and this reduced demand for the types of services provided by Entwistle's criminal element. Today the hamlet of Entwistle, named after James Entwistle, is known for its 270.6-metre (902-foot) railway bridge spanning the Pembina River.

In 1909, the Canadian Northern Railway (CNR) neared Entwistle and built its own bridge, made of steel, over the river; by 1917, however, 129 kilometres of track near Obed were removed to provide steel for the war effort, and the CNR steel bridge was dismantled. You can still see the bridge's eight concrete pilings along Pembina Provincial Park's day-use road.

Train on bridge in Pembina River Provincial Park

JOAN MARIE GALAT

DRAYTON VALLEY

Directions: Exit Edmonton on Hwy 16 west, take the Hwy 22 south exit toward Drayton Valley and Entwistle, keep left at the fork, and follow the signs for Hwy 22 south.

Distance: 145 km, or about 1 hour and 45 minutes, from Edmonton.

Info: Brazeau Regional Tourism Visitor Information Centre is located at 6009–44th Avenue. 780-542-7529 or 1-800-633-0899.

The earliest pioneers in the Drayton Valley area began breaking land in 1907. Dora and William Drake, along with their six-year-old daughter, Dolly, were the first to homestead here. The settlement was called Powerhouse because of a plan to build a dam roughly 9.6 kilometres south, but the scheme was abandoned when World War I broke out. Upon opening the area's first post office, the Drakes discovered "Powerhouse" had already been used and renamed the community Drayton Valley.

Many of the area's first pioneers worked as trappers until fur prices dropped in 1920. Others harvested lumber, and in 1930, approximately 350 men worked in 30 lumber camps and floated logs downstream on the North Saskatchewan River to Edmonton. By 1945, the forests were harvested and mixed farming became the most common way to support a family.

Life changed forever in 1953 when Mobil Oil discovered what became North America's largest oil find: the Pembina Oil Field. The area boomed as more than 70 oil companies came to Drayton Valley, and the population expanded from 75 to 2,000 people in one year. Drayton Valley changed rapidly with the arrival of prostitutes, around-the-clock saloons, and people living in skid shacks—weathered buildings lining a 1-kilometre rutted dirt road. The community became a town in 1957.

Today it's a pleasant drive to Drayton Valley—the largest community in Brazeau County and home to 6,893 people. Fields scattered with pumpjacks lead to town, which sits atop a gorgeous plateau between the North Saskatchewan and Pembina rivers.

When you arrive, follow the signs to the Omniplex (5737–45th Avenue) for an up-close look at a large pumpjack painted in the town colours. The Lion's West Valley Park is here and includes a day-use area with picnic tables. Drayton Valley features more than 14 kilometres of pathways that connect all town parks and lead into the countryside. The Rotary/Pembina Nordic Community Trails range in length from less than 1 kilometre to almost 3 kilometres, and are suitable for walking, mountain biking, or cross-country skiing.

The annual Thunder in the Valley Drag Races are a North Peace Bracket Race Association (NPBRA) circuit stop. For information, call 780-514-2200. Other annual events include the Drayton Valley Bench Fair, Snowmobile Snow Drags, Rapid Fire Motor Sports Show, and Sprint Car Platinum Cup Races; there are also rodeos, livestock shows, and light-horse competitions.

Dedicated to presenting area history, the Drayton Valley Museum is located in the Lion's West Valley Park, just off Highway 22 at the west entrance to the Drayton Valley RV Park, Omniplex, and Lion's Rodeo Grounds. The museum is open from 1 p.m. to 4 p.m. on Wednesdays, but groups may book a tour at any time by calling in advance. Phone Charlie Miner of the Drayton Valley Historical Society at 780-542-5482.

If you would like to look at some fine Canadian art, visit one of the town's two free public galleries. Throughout the year, the Hamdon Art Gallery displays a number of collections by Canadian artists using different mediums. The gallery is located at the new MacKenzie Conference Centre located at the Omniplex, and is open from 8:30 a.m. to 4:30 p.m. on weekdays. (780-514-2200.)

Em-Te Town

Location: 59 km from Drayton Valley. Exit Drayton Valley on Hwy 2 south, turn west at the Em-Te Town sign, and travel 10 km.
Info: Admission charged. Trail-riding helmets are mandatory; bring your own or rent one. 780-388-2166; www.emtetown.com.

Em-Te Town is a privately built western ghost town, complete with a jailhouse, harness shop, livery stable, bank, church, restaurant, swinging bridge, and the Hogs Breath Saloon. It has been used as a western setting for a number of television and film projects, including a McDonald's commercial shot in the summer of 1992.

Visitors can enjoy a petting barn, trail and wagon rides, picnic area, and fully licensed saloon and restaurant. There are areas for riding snowmobiles and all-terrain vehicles. You can also go cross-country skiing or sit back and enjoy a sleigh ride.

Brazeau Reservoir Provincial Recreation Area

Location: 60 km southwest of Drayton Valley on Hwy 620.
Info: The reservoir offers pleasant boating for canoes, kayaks, and boats powered by small engines, but be careful to avoid driftwood and snags just below the water's surface. 780-894-0006.

A tributary of the North Saskatchewan River, the Brazeau River is named after Joseph E. Brazeau, a Hudson's Bay Company clerk and postmaster who worked in Edmonton, Jasper, and Rocky Mountain House between 1852 and 1864. Built for hydroelectric purposes, the 120-metre dam has controlled the river's flow since 1964. Every year the plant generates enough electricity to meet the needs of the equivalent of 56,285 Alberta homes.

The boreal lower foothills eco-region that includes the 131 hectares (323 acres) of the Brazeau Reservoir Provincial Recreation Area contains predominantly coniferous and mixed-wood forest, which represents a transition from true boreal to subalpine regions. Lodgepole pine stands are most common, followed by trembling aspen and less-frequent groupings of balsam poplar. Black spruce, Labrador tea, and sphagnum moss populate the areas around the region's many bogs, and poorly drained peat lands give rise to sedge fens.

Look for moose, elk, mule deer, and white-tailed deer, as well as cavity nesting birds, such as tree swallows, and common goldeneye. Great blue herons nest here, as do about 15 osprey—the province's greatest concentration of nesting osprey. Watch for these birds near the nesting platforms installed on power poles, and walk along the south edge of the canal for especially fine birdwatching.

The Brazeau River is home to a significant number of boreal forest bird species at the limit of their southern range. Look for the sandhill crane, boreal owl, greater yellowlegs, and Philadelphia vireo. A search of the shallow water below may reveal lurking northern pike.

Attractive for its wildlife watching opportunities, this area appeals to those who enjoy canoeing, kayaking, swimming, fishing, sailing, powerboating, and windsurfing. There is a boat ramp, fish-cleaning station, interpretive viewpoint, pit toilets, and shelters—both with and without a cook stove.

BRETON

Directions: Exit Edmonton on Hwy 2 south, take exit 517 for Hwy 39 west toward Drayton Valley; merge onto Hwy 39, and turn left at Hwy 20.
Distance: 108 km, or about 1 hour and 28 minutes, from Edmonton.
Info: www.village.breton.ab.ca.

In 1908, the Canadian government encouraged the flow of Black American settlers from Oklahoma. In addition to harsh weather, isolation, and all the other hardships that came with settling in Alberta, many who arrived here also faced discrimination. Keystone, now called the village of Breton, was one of four rural Alberta communities founded by Black settlers from Oklahoma and neighbouring states during the early 20th century. Today Breton is home to 550 people.

Breton and District Historical Museum

Location: 4711–51st Street, in the former Breton Elementary School, Breton.
Info: Open daily from July through August, 11 a.m. to 5 p.m. Museum personnel are happy to open for private off-season tours. 780-696-2551; bretonmuse@yahoo.com.

Email is checked almost daily, but leave a phone message well in advance because messages are not checked daily. Admission by donation.

The Breton and District Historical Museum is housed in a two-room school built in 1948. The museum focuses on Black history, as well as lumbering, community, and agricultural development. Every February, the museum hosts a Black History Day. The Keystone Cemetery contains a cairn honouring its Black settlers.

COYOTE LAKE NATURAL AREA

Directions: Exit Edmonton on Hwy 2 south. Turn right (west) on Hwy 39 towards Calmar. Continue west onto Hwy 622, which turns into Township Road 500. Drive past St. Francis and turn south on Range Road 44. Parking is available near McIntyre Meadow at the nature sanctuary.
Distance: 100 km southwest of Edmonton.
Info: 1-877-262-1253; www.natureconservancy.ca.

Coyote Lake sits in one of Alberta's richest biological areas. It is situated in a transition zone between dry mixed-wood boreal forest and parkland. The natural area supports more than 22 mammal species, 154 types of birds—9 of which are imperiled—and 266 different plants, including a number of rare and uncommon orchids. Coyote Lake provides important feeding habitat for great blue herons, resting sites for numerous migrating waterfowl, and nesting habitat for the red-necked grebe, common loon, and ring-necked duck. The absence of insecticide spraying in recent years has allowed bird populations to increase dramatically.

The 130-hectare (320 acre) nature sanctuary and 194-hectare (480 acre) conservation area are situated on land donated to the Nature Conservancy of Canada in 1996. The nature sanctuary is open for daytime visits and self-guided hikes. Interpretive walks are available to groups who book ahead. Group walks and guided tours are available by prior arrangement through the Nature Conservancy (see Info).

PIGEON LAKE

Directions: Exit Edmonton on Hwy 2 south. Take exit 482B to reach Hwy 13 (west).
Distance: 88 km, or about 1 hour and 8 minutes, from Edmonton.
Info: www.pigeonlake.com.

A large, shallow lake, Pigeon Lake may have been named for the vast flocks of passenger pigeons once common here. The lake's Cree name is *Hmi-hmoo*—meaning "Woodpecker Lake." For hundreds of years, Aboriginal people used a trail on Pigeon Lake's northwest shore and took advantage of an artesian well along the path.

Formerly of Liverpool, England, Methodist missionary Reverend Robert Rundle travelled through the Pigeon Lake area in 1845. He initially came to Edmonton in 1840 to serve the Aboriginal people and work as company chaplain at Edmonton House—the original Fort Edmonton—located where the Sturgeon River flows into the North Saskatchewan River, just north of modern-day Fort Saskatchewan. Rundle found the Aboriginal people interacted very differently when he met them at their own camps rather than at Fort Edmonton, and he requested permission to establish a mission outside the Hudson's Bay Company fort.

His request was approved, and Rundle chose to locate the new mission on the northwest shore of Pigeon Lake because of its abundant supply of fish and the clean water that continually flowed from the artesian well. He knew the land was fertile, for he had tested it and found it suitable for agriculture. Rundle considered it an ideal place to conduct missionary work and to work toward his dream to help the Aboriginal people grow their own provisions. He established the Rundle Mission in 1847—a time when food shortages were an increasing concern. The original mission consisted of a few log buildings clustered around the well. Rundle introduced syllabics to the Cree who came to the mission, which enabled them to read and write in their own language for the first time. Nakoda, Cree, and missionaries continued to meet here for nearly 50 years. You can see a National Historic Monument that was dedicated to Rev. Robert

COLLEEN LOMAS

1967 Historic Monument dedicated to Rev. Robert Rundle at Rundle's Mission, Pigeon Lake

Rundle in 1967, and visit the Benjamin and Margaret Sinclair Alberta Historic Site, where the stories of residents and visitors are told along the self-guiding interpretive trail. Access the beach across the road from the mission or visit the public Mission Beach 0.5 kilometres down the road.

Pigeon Lake's west shore is also historically significant. It was home to a Hudson's Bay Company trading post that closed only seven years after its 1868 opening. Commercial fishing, logging, and farming helped settlers get by in the early 1900s, but today Pigeon Lake is known for its recreational appeal.

In addition to restaurants and a number of other services, The Village at Pigeon Lake offers a charming boardwalk of country shops to wander through, including an irresistible bakery at the Village Market. Upon entering the store, look for the photograph display showing local homesteaders, as well as the hand-hewn replica of the original Crystal Springs Store. (For more information, visit www.villageatpigeonlake.com.) Community events include tailgate sales, annual dogsled races, and an ice-golf tournament.

COLLEEN LOMAS

Historic boardwalk at Rundle's Mission, Pigeon Lake

In addition to trails within the provincial park, Pigeon Lake has walking paths through an 89-hectare (220 acre) nature reserve adjacent to Rundle's Mission. You can stop for a picnic on the hill overlooking Pigeon Lake, where you will find an outdoor toilet and the always-open Telfordville Church. There is a small group shelter and firepits on the east side of Memorial Lodge, which can be used by the public when not booked by a group.

Mulhurst Bay on the north side of Pigeon Lake has a small beach area and boat launch. You can reach it on Highway 771 north—a 10-minute drive from The Village at Pigeon Lake.

Winter visitors will appreciate the area's cross-country ski trails. There are 13 kilometres of non-groomed trails at Pigeon Lake Family Park on Highway 771 north, 10 minutes from The Village at Pigeon Lake.

Ma-Me-O Beach

Location: At the south end of Pigeon Lake on Hwy 13A.
Info: www.pigeonlake.com.

The Summer Village of Ma-Me-O Beach is located on Pigeon Lake's south end and takes its name from the Cree *Ma-Me-O*, meaning "white pigeon." Ma-Me-O boasts a sandy beach with shallow water that is ideal for young children. You can swim here or take sailing lessons. Amenities include changing and toilet facilities, picnic shelters, docks, boat launches, and playgrounds, as well as a concession. The village has a tennis court, along with a town hall where bingos, flea markets, and family dances are held.

Pigeon Lake Provincial Park

Location: 5 km northwest of the village at Pigeon Lake. From The Village at Pigeon Lake, travel west on Hwy 13 and turn right (north) on Hwy 771.
Info: 780-586-2644.

Designated in 1967, Pigeon Lake Provincial Park is an extremely popular place to enjoy outdoor recreation close to Edmonton. The park provides opportunities for swimming, canoeing, kayaking, waterskiing, fishing, hiking, powerboating, windsurfing, and horseshoes. You will find boat ramps, change rooms, fish-cleaning stations, and toilets, as well as a playground, horseshoe pitch, concession, and grocery store. Wildlife viewing and birdwatching opportunities abound. Golf courses, shopping, and a farmers' market are within a 15-minute drive of the park. Winter activities include cross-country skiing, ice fishing, and dogsled tours.

Zeiner Park is just 6 kilometres past the provincial park. It has a sandy beach, playground, concession, boat rentals, firepits, picnic tables, volleyball, and showers.

WIZARD LAKE JUBILEE PARK

Directions: Exit Edmonton on Hwy 2 south, take exit 517 to reach Hwy 39 west heading toward Drayton Valley/Calmar; drive through Calmar (50th Avenue) and turn left at 50th Street/Hwy 795, turn right at Hwy 616, turn left at 30th Street/

Range Road 281, and turn right at Wizard Lake Road.

Distance: 84.8 km, or about 1 hour and 16 minutes, from Edmonton.

Info: Posted speed limits on the lake restrict boats in some areas.

The drive to Wizard Lake takes you through the town of Calmar, about 42 kilometres southwest of Edmonton. C. G. Blomquist, the town's first postmaster, named the community in 1900 in honour of his home town, Kalmar, Sweden.

Nearby, the long and winding Wizard Lake lies in a forested, deep glacial meltwater channel formed before the last glaciation. Water flows from the lake to the North Saskatchewan River through Conjuring Creek, which was named by early Aboriginal people whose legends told of unusual sounds coming from magical beings in the lake. Until the late 1960s, the lake was commonly called Conjuring Lake.

The valley shelters the lake from the wind, making the water's surface a dream for those who enjoy water sports. Wizard Lake Jubilee Park has a beach, playground, and boat launch.

The Wizard Waterski and Wakeboard Club maintains a site at the lake and runs annual events, recreational tournaments, and one ratings tournament—the Wizard World Cup. Ski clinics for skiers with disabilities are held on Monday nights from June until the end of August. Visit www.wizardwaterski.com for more information.

CHIP LAKE PARK

Directions: Exit Edmonton on Hwy 16 west, turn north onto Green Court Road (Range Road 92) to Township Road 544 and travel 11 km (5 miles) west. All roads are signed.

Distance: 135 km, or about 1 hour and 30 minutes, from Edmonton.

Info: Wheelchair accessible. 780-325-2460.

Once called Buffalo Chip or Buffalo Dung Lake, Chip Lake offers a beautiful spot to launch a canoe and places to fish. Birders will appreciate the park's plethora of songbirds and waterfowl. There are

127 recorded bird species, including whooping cranes and osprey. Northern pygmy owls are known to nest at Chip Lake and although these secretive birds like to hide in thick cover, you may be able to spot one at the very top of a tree. They are most active and most commonly heard between dawn and dusk; listen for their repetitive series of whistled hoots "too-too-too-too-too-too-too."

Park amenities include a day-use area, picnic shelter, boat launch, and playground. A music festival is held here on the last weekend of May.

EDSON

Directions: Exit Edmonton on Hwy 16 west.
Distance: 202 km, or about 2 hours and 15 minutes, from Edmonton.
Info: www.townofedson.ca.

The town of Edson marks the trailhead from which early settlers once travelled through the Peace River Valley and on to the North. Before the town existed, the trailhead site was chosen to serve as a Grand Trunk Pacific Railway divisional point. Surveyors marked the townsite and 15 people settled here when the tracks were laid in August 1910. The area was advertised as a booming place to live, and lots selling for $200 were suddenly valued at more than $1,000. In 1911, the population grew from 490 people in January to 1,200 residents that summer. The same year, clay marl, used for making cement, was discovered west of Edson, and a plant in nearby Marlboro opened, with cement being shipped to Edmonton and more distant locations. Clay, for use in cosmetics, was also mined from McLeod River deposits in 1934.

The region's first post office was called Heatherwood but was later named after the general manager and eventual president of the Grand Trunk Pacific Railroad: Edson J. Chamberlain.

Edson was officially incorporated in 1911, and between 1911 and 1915, travellers aiming to reach Grande Prairie took the Edson Trail. The province of Alberta hired crews of men to cut a path through the forest; they cut their way through the forest with axes to create a 400-kilometre overland route across continuous stretches of muskeg and deep mud. When rutted mud on the trail dried, wagons swayed precariously, which prompted many passengers to walk rather than ride. Travellers faced a difficult route, and many individuals drowned while trying to transport their belongings across the perilous waters at one of four major river crossings. The unforgiving trail was gradually improved with the introduction of rest areas and ferries. Hay was also stored for animal feed. The introduction of the Edmonton, Dunvegan, and British Columbia Railway (EDBC) made the trail redundant in 1916.

Today the Yellowhead Trans-Canada Highway passes through Edson. Its name comes from the Iroquois trapper and guide Pierre Bostonais, who was nicknamed "Tête Jaune," French for "yellow head," because of his light-coloured hair. In 1825, Bostonais accompanied James Macmillan, a Hudson's Bay Company employee who had been sent to survey a low pass across the continental divide near Jasper House. The two men were seeking a route to transport dressed leather to New Caledonia—the area now known as central British Columbia. New Caledonia had little in the way of large game and needed leather to make sturdy moccasins for Aboriginal trappers. Also called Leather Track and Leather Pass, Yellowhead is the name that has endured.

About 8,000 vehicles pass through Edson daily on the Trans-Canada Yellowhead Highway. The community is home to the world's largest ballpark, two museums, two cross-country ski trail systems, and many outdoor recreational opportunities. The region's rich natural resources—oil, gas, coal, and timber—help support a population of 8,365 residents.

Annual events include the Mooseheart Loppet Family Fun Cross Country Race in March, the Holy Redeemer Drama Festival in April, the Medicine Lodge Rodeo in May, Canada Day Celebrations on July 1, Chamber of Commerce Sidewalk Jamboree in August, and a Santa Claus Parade in December.

Location: Turn left onto 53rd Street from Hwy 16 west, Edson.

Info: The visitor information centre is open Monday through Friday, 8 a.m. to 4 p.m., from September through April; Monday through Friday, 8 a.m. to 7 p.m., from May to September. The centre is open on Saturday, Sunday, and statutory holidays from 10 a.m. to 6 p.m. The Galloway Station Museum is open daily from May through September, 10 a.m. to 5 p.m. There is a small admission charge.

You will know you have reached Centennial Park when you see the mounted Lockheed T33 jet along the Yellowhead Highway. This popular stopping point is a good place to walk around and relax. Be sure to take a stroll to the giant water fountain along Bench Creek and enjoy the park's ponds, waterfalls, and bridges. The park is home to a 1907 Canadian National caboose, which is one of the oldest CN relics exhibited in Canada. You will also find the Edson & District

JOAN MARIE GALAT

Lockheed T33, in Centennial Park, Edson

Chamber of Commerce, visitor information centre, and Galloway Station Museum. The latter displays industrial artifacts from the railway, coal mining, and lumber sectors. Call 780-723-5696 for more information.

Red Brick Arts Centre

Location: 4818–7th Avenue, Edson.
Info: Open Monday to Friday, 9 a.m. to 4:30 p.m. (closed from noon to 1 p.m.). 780-723-3582. Admission by donation. Wheelchair accessible.

The Red Brick Arts Centre is a registered historic resource that will interest visitors of all ages. Restored and renovated, the 1913 school building is Edson's central point for artistic and cultural events throughout the year. It is home to the Hatlen Theatre, dance studios, an art gallery, and a gift shop. You can tour the School Room Museum and perhaps enjoy a butter- or ice-cream–making demonstration, or watch how clothes are cleaned using a washboard.

Fickle Lake Provincial Recreation Area

Location: 39 km southwest of Edson, off Hwy 47.
Info: Open May 1 to mid-October. Powerboat speed limit in posted areas is 12 km per hour. 780-797-4154.

Fickle Lake is a popular fishing spot and offers a pleasant place to paddle a kayak or canoe. The roped swimming area is on the east side of the lake. Despite the chilly water, it is a favourite spot for children who enjoy shallow water and building sandcastles. For a hike that will take about an hour, follow the signs to the old trapper shack—Elkoff's Cabin.

Recreation area amenities include a boat launch, picnic tables, firepits, free firewood, fish-cleaning station, and pit toilets. In addition to the main pier, boaters will find a couple of smaller landing areas along the lake.

MAYERTHORPE

Directions: Exit Edmonton on Hwy 16 west, then take Hwy 43 north.
Distance: 137 km, or about 1 hour and 34 minutes, from Edmonton.
Info: www.townofmayerthorpe.ab.ca.

On the way to Mayerthorpe, pull into Sangudo for a look at the world's largest working sundial, which is shaped like a grain elevator. You might also enjoy stopping at the Paddle River Dam, which has a day-use area with a boat launch. It's a pretty spot to drop a fishing line, swim, and water-ski. Winter visitors are often seen ice-fishing here. The Rochfort Bridge Trading Post is also along Highway 43. From the trading post, you can view the Rochfort Bridge by heading north on Highway 43, then west toward Township Road 570C, followed by a sharp right at Township Road 572 (totalling 12.8 kilometres from the Rochfort Bridge Trading Post). The longest wooden trestle bridge in western Canada, Rochfort Bridge spans about 736 metres (2,414 feet). The nearby Rochfort Bridge Trading Post has a licensed dining room with homestyle cooking. Ask about the 1-pound hamburger: if you can eat it in 20 minutes, it's free. The Trading Post gift shop, with its unique country gifts and crafts, is a fun place to browse.

Like many Alberta towns, Mayerthorpe takes part of its name from an early postmaster, Robert Ingersoll Mayer, who moved to Alberta with his wife, Emma, in 1908. Peter Gunn, Member of the Legislative Assembly, suggested the name Mayerville when opening the post office, but Mayerthorpe—formed by adding the family name of a local teacher—was chosen instead.

In 1919, the Canadian Northern Railway was on its way. Leo Oscar Crockett, a US navy veteran turned settler, subdivided land and encouraged pioneers to live in the townsite of Little Paddle, about 5 kilometres east of Mayer's post office. In 1921, the first post office closed and a new one opened in Little Paddle, which took the name Mayerthorpe. Incorporated as a village in 1927, the community became a town in 1961.

Today the town of Mayerthorpe has 1,474 residents. Located in the midst of farm and cattle country, it is primarily an agricultural hub with a mix of oil, gas, and forestry industries. It is also the official start of the 640-kilometre (397.6 mile) Cowboy Trail that stretches south to Cardston.

Local attractions include the Mayerthorpe Elevator Museum, housed in one of Alberta's few remaining wooden grain elevators. It is being restored as a museum to honour the area's agricultural history. Lessard Lake, Rangeton Park, and secluded Dolberg Lake are recreational areas worthy of exploration. Annual events include a rodeo, the 4H Beef Show and Sale, Show and Shine, and Agricultural Fair. The Rangeton Farmers Day Festival is held at a nearby rustic campground beside the Pembina River.

Located where the ferry once crossed the river, the Ol' Pembina River Ferry Crossing is an RV park with a day-use area for visitors. Check out the museum of local settler artifacts and the Coca-Cola-themed 1950s soda shop. Antique and vintage cars and trucks are displayed, as is an antique and classic tractor collection with more than 60 tractors. Admission is by donation, and there is a $2 per person charge to use the cook house area. (780-785-2379.)

Fallen Four Memorial Park

Location: 4602–52nd Street, Mayerthorpe.
Info: 780-786-2033; info@fallenfour.ca.

The Fallen Four Memorial Park honours four Mayerthorpe RCMP members who lost their lives on March 3, 2005. Constables Peter Schiemann, Brock Myrol, Leo Johnston, and Anthony Gordon were shot following a raid of a marijuana-growing operation on a farm near Mayerthorpe. It was the force's greatest loss of life in a single day in more than 100 years.

The memorial also commemorates all peace officers in Canada killed in the line of duty. The park's design centres on the number four—four officers, the four winds, and the four directional points

Fallen Four Memorial Park, Mayerthorpe

on a compass—to symbolize the RCMP's influence throughout the country. Life-size bronze statues of the fallen officers face outward toward each of the compass's directional points. Studio West Ltd., from Cochrane, AB, created and cast the centre obelisk and the bronze statues of the officers after consulting with family members to ensure their similarity to the four fallen officers.

The park is home to a 270-square-metre facility containing the visitor information centre (780-786-2033), as well as a small museum, donor-appreciation wall, and gift shop. The grand opening took place July 4, 2008. You will find a day-use picnic area and playground here, as well as concrete benches and picnic tables situated along landscaped areas and walking paths. Be sure to note the prairie skyline from the gazebo.

WHITECOURT

Directions: Exit Edmonton on Hwy 16 west, turn north onto Hwy 43.
Distance: 181 km, or about 2 hours, from Edmonton.
Info: www.whitecourt.ca.

Whitecourt's first inhabitants, the Woodland Cree, called the area *Sagitawah*—"where the waters meet"—because four waterways come together on the eastern border of the Rocky Mountain foothills: the Athabasca River, McLeod River, Sakwatemau (Eagle) River, and Beaver Creek. Whitecourt is located at the convergence of the Athabasca and McLeod rivers.

Early explorers and residents used these rivers for transportation, and in 1897 the Hudson's Bay Company (HBC) built a trading post near the present-day location of the Whitecourt Golf and Country Club. Some of the Klondike gold prospectors who stopped here to collect supplies and rest later returned as settlers.

By 1908 the Whitecourt region was finally surveyed into quarter sections. For $10 settlers could file for land. Some signed for land they had squatted on; others purchased land they had not yet seen. Title ownership required spending six months of three consecutive years living on and farming the property. Aiming to lure pioneers west, the Canadian government advertised heavily in Europe and the US, but poor transportation routes meant difficult travel. One family en route to Whitecourt from Edmonton took four weeks to make the trip. Settlers often worked on roads in return for tax deductions.

When a post office was established in 1910, some settlers wanted the community to be called Sagitawah or McLeod River Flats. Instead, it was registered as Whitecourt, presumably after mail carrier Walter White from Greencourt—the location where Whitecourt's mail had originally been sent. Having expected that they would be able to vote on the town's name, residents were upset, but they let the name Whitecourt stand to avoid slowing post office approval.

Train service became available in 1921, providing one-day service to Edmonton. Because of the railroad, the lumber industry began to thrive and more settlers came to the region.

Today Whitecourt's population is nearing 8,800 residents. With 11,000 square kilometres of forest surrounding the town, the area offers seemingly unlimited opportunities for outdoor enthusiasts, and the town is known as the Snowmobile Capital of Alberta. The rivers are ideal for those who enjoy paddling a canoe or kayak, boating, and fishing. Many enjoy tubing down the McLeod River. (Ask at

the Whitecourt and District Forest Interpretive Centre visitor information for a map, conditions, and directions.)

The town of Whitecourt has 30 kilometres of trails, including
6 kilometres of paved pathways that connect residential, downtown,
and forested areas between the valley and hilltop. The surrounding
area has hundreds of kilometres of trails designated for off-highway
vehicles.

If you are interested in picnicking in town, visit Friendship Park,
which recognizes the bond between Whitecourt and its twin town,
Kamiyubetsu, Japan. Riverboat Park on Whitecourt's west edge has a
picnic area, shelter, and boat launch that provides access to both the
McLeod and Athabasca rivers. Centennial Park, on Whitecourt's south
boundary, is a large green space with numerous walking trails. Rotary
Park (51st Street) has areas for picnicking, sports fields, playgrounds,
and an asphalt trail with historical story boards around a pond. Fishing is permitted from May to October, but is limited to individuals
younger than 16 years of age and those accompanying these children.
Be sure to check out the unique Whitecourt River Slide—a creek built
for tubing and play, with pools and drops leading to a shallow basin
and beach.

Whitecourt and District Forest Interpretive Centre and Heritage Park

Location: 3002–33rd Street (west side of Hwy 43 on Whitecourt's south end).
Info: Tourist information is located in the Forest Interpretive Centre foyer. From
July 1 to August 31, open Monday to Friday, 9 a.m. to 6 p.m., and on weekends,
11 a.m. to 6 p.m. From September 1 through June 30, open Monday to Friday,
9 a.m. to 5 p.m. Gallery admission charged. 1-800-313-7383, 780-778-5363,
or 780-778-2214.

Built with open-beam construction and a tipi design, the Forest Interpretive Gallery is a beautiful place to discover how sustainable forestry has affected the development of the Whitecourt area, which has
two sawmills, a medium-density fibreboard (MDF) plant, a market
pulp mill, and an integrated pulp and newsprint mill.

The $1.7-million facility provides hands-on exhibits, audio-visual presentations, artifacts displays, and self-guided tours that examine the boreal forest's future, along with the past, present, and future of Alberta's forestry industry. It looks at Aboriginal people's relationship with the forest, the consequences of settlement and other development issues, and the economic impact of forestry. The 657-square-metre centre includes a multimedia museum gallery, an 80-seat auditorium, and a gift shop with locally crafted products.

Heritage Park features three visitor-accessible buildings—Blue Ridge's old United Church, an original log home called Baxter Cabin, and a re-created trapper's shack. You will also find a collection of antique vehicles and farm machinery, as well as a barn. Take a heritage building tour to discover some surprising facts about these buildings' significance in Whitecourt history.

The forest around the centre is used as a model to illustrate the importance of keeping homes safe from potential forest fires. An 800-metre trail includes interpretive signs explaining fire safety.

GUIDED INDUSTRY TOURS

The Whitecourt and District Chamber of Commerce, in partnership with the Alberta Newsprint Company and Millar Western Forest Products, offers free guided tours. Depending on current plant operations, tours are available during summer months on weekdays from 9 a.m. to 5 p.m. Book a day ahead, or come to the tourist information centre early in the morning. You can make tour arrangements by contacting Whitecourt's tourist information at 1-800-313-7383, 780-778-5363, or 780-778-2214.

Alberta Newsprint Company

Location: 10 km northwest of Whitecourt. Travel on Hwy 43 north to the Hwy 32 junction; turn left onto the marked Alberta Newsprint Company (ANC) access road; travel about 1 km to enter the main parking lot.

The province's only papermaking facility, the Alberta Newsprint Company produces about 720 metric tons of newsprint each day or 260,000 metric tons per year, which translates to approximately 1,400 metres per minute, or 84 kilometres each hour. The paper is made from 95 percent thermo-chemical pulp that uses sawmill waste residuals and 5 percent recycled content from de-inked newspapers and magazines. Tours show the papermaking process from start to finish.

Millar Western Forest Products

Location: 5004–52nd Street, Whitecourt, at the confluence of the Athabasca and McLeod rivers.

The $40 million Millar Western sawmill in Whitecourt opened in 2001. A single-line sawmill, it produces dimensional lumber using more than 7,000 logs in an eight-hour shift. Every year, about 900,000 cubic metres of tree length are brought in and cut to length to produce more than 200 million board feet of kiln-dried lumber—enough to erect 11,000 average-size single-family homes. The tour shows visitors the daily operations involved in running the mill.

Eric S. Huestis Demonstration Forest

Location: About 13 km north of Whitecourt on Hwy 32.
Info: The front gate is open from May to October. 780-778-7267.

Visit the 10-square-kilometre Eric S. Huestis Demonstration Forest for a great hike and see how a forest can be managed to provide recreation opportunities, wildlife habitat, and harvesting over an extended time period. Established in the late 1980s, the Huestis Demonstration Forest includes five cutblocks (i.e., a specified area authorized for logging) of aspen, pine, spruce, mixed wood, and exotic species. Until recently, industrial activity such as oil and gas production has been limited here. A 7-kilometre trek leads past 26 interpretive sites that illustrate stages of forest life. You can see the impact of forestry and talk to interpretive staff.

ALGAE IN ALBERTA LAKES

Algal blooms have occurred in Alberta lakes for centuries. Because they can produce liver toxins and neurotoxins that can be deadly if swallowed, it is wise to familiarize yourself with some algal facts.

Make sure to stay out of water with an algal bloom or visible scum within 1 metre of a lake's surface. Although not every algal bloom is toxic, some varieties cause rashes and hives. Keep pets out of algal blooms and make sure they do not drink lake water. Toxins take time to break down, so wait at least two weeks after a bloom disappears before entering the water.

Every July, Alberta lakes warm up, and sometimes reach 25 degrees Celsius—the perfect temperature for maximum blue-green algae growth. Warmer temperatures swell growth, and high total phosphorus concentrations, caused by low dissolved oxygen concentrations over bottom sediments, contribute to the problem.

As blue-green algae forms thin layers near a lake's surface, wind and waves move the bloom toward shore, where it collects and decomposes, producing a strong odour. Algal blooms vary from year to year, depending on nutrient availability, air and water temperatures, overall sunlight, and wind velocity. A lake that experiences blooms one year may improve in subsequent years.

Carson-Pegasus Provincial Park

Location: 24 km north of Whitecourt. Exit Whitecourt on Hwy 43, turn north at Hwy 32, and follow the signs to reach the park entrance.
Info: The maximum powerboat speed is 12 km per hour. All boats are prohibited in some posted areas. 780-778-2664.

Carson-Pegasus Provincial Park encompasses McLeod Lake, once known as Carson Lake, and Little McLeod Lake, and was previously called, simply, Pegasus. Until the early 20th century, this area was significant to Aboriginal peoples living near the lake. Members of the Stoney, Woodland Cree, and possibly Beaver tribes came here for the lake's abundant fish.

Formerly an Alberta Forest Service campground, Carson-Pegasus became a provincial park in 1982. It is an especially popular spot for catching rainbow trout. The presence of a seawall makes fishing convenient for shore anglers. The park contains mixed-wood forests of aspen, balsam poplar, balsam fir, and white spruce, as well as willow and alder along the shorelines. There are black spruce bogs, and sedge-grass marshes and fens. Both boreal and foothill bird species are attracted to this habitat, with more than 113 bird species recorded and 106 species breeding here. The lake is also a popular resting place for waterfowl en route during spring and fall migration.

Open year-round, Carson-Pegasus Provincial Park provides opportunities for swimming, birding, canoeing, kayaking, fishing, power-boating, and wildlife viewing. Facilities include a boat ramp, fish-cleaning station, hand launch, pier, toilets, playground, and shelter with stove, as well as a picnic area, convenience store, and boat rentals. In winter, trails are groomed for cross-country skiing. You can also go snowshoeing, tobogganing, and ice fishing. A warm-up shelter is available.

Help preserve all natural settings by staying on designated trails, boardwalks, and viewing platforms. Watch wildlife from a distance, and avoid nesting sites. Please do not disturb animals, pick flowers, remove plants, or disrupt the wildlife viewing activities of others.

PHONE NUMBERS

Alberta's Lakeland: 1-888-645-4155
AMA Road Reports: 1-877-AMA-HWYS (1-877-262-4997)
Athabasca Country Tourism: 1-877-211-8669
Cowboy Trail Tourism Association: 1-866-627-3051
Environment Canada Weather: 780-468-4940
Iron Horse Trail: 1-888-645-4155
Kalyna Country: 1-888-452-5962
Provincial Parks and Recreation areas: 780-427-3582,
    or 1-866-427-3582
Tourism Red Deer: 1-800-215-8946
Travel Alberta: 1-800-ALBERTA (1-800-252-3782)

HOLIDAYS

Victoria Day weekend: third weekend in May
Canada Day: July 1
August long weekend: first weekend in August
Labour Day weekend: first weekend in September

ACKNOWLEDGEMENTS

Compiling a travel guide requires the input of a great many individuals and organizations. In fear of inadvertently omitting any one name, I offer a collective thank you to the many professionals who answered my questions, provided photos, reviewed content, and took the time to provide feedback and suggestions. This includes staff and volunteers who work for or who are involved with Alberta towns, cities, counties, chambers of commerce, provincial parks, recreation areas, historic venues, and other attractions. It also encompasses friends from different regions who provided useful information, particularly Janis Schole.

I offer a special thank you to the Writers Guild of Alberta and Library Association of Alberta, who organized and sponsored the writer-in-residence program, which placed me in the Yellowhead Regional Library. This three-month period provided a portion of much-appreciated writing time, which I dedicated to this book. The residency also gave me opportunities to travel to the library region's rural areas, which cover parts of the Edmonton day-trips zone.

Thank you also to my parents, who instilled a love of picnicking on our many travels, and to Grant Wiens for accompanying me on my explorations, and for helping me sort through maps and other materials.

My appreciation extends to editor Brendan Wild, who knows the importance of a well-placed comma, to Leslie Bell for the maps, and to the Whitecap Books staff, who contributed enthusiastically to this project, making it an exciting endeavour in every way.

INDEX